12/15/05
To Pat Dumas,
Much Success as
you strive
to Overcome
adversity!
Lenell Geter

Overcome, Succeed & Prosper

The 5 Attitudes for Success to Enable Individuals or Families to Lead Successful Lives

by Lenell Geter

The Marzinza Publishing Group
Columbia, South Carolina

Powerful Testimonies about Overcome, Succeed and Prosper

"Lenell Geter has done a masterful job of integrating his personal experiences with his spiritual walk with God to provide us with this outstanding book on the family. As you read this book, you will become encouraged by Lenell's understanding of purpose and passion for his life to help our families. This book renews our hope for disintegrating families and broken homes."

—Charles B. Jackson, Sr., B.S., M.Div., D.D. , Senior Pastor Brookland Baptist Church

"The positive in this case is his program of Psycho-Cultivation, a five-step plan for overcoming adversity and using it as the 'fertilizer for future growth and success'. Lenell shares his powerful belief in the potential everyone has to rise above the problems that befall them, as long as they believe they can do so. His words are powerful since he has what he advocates."

—Vicki Phillips, Author of Personal Development

"Lenell Geter, who knows despair and the vagaries of justice better than anyone I can think of , has written a valuable guide for Americans, regardless of their age. It was Mr. Geter's firm faith in his God, in human decency and in his own wonderfully crafted principles, that carried him through the toughest of challenges."

—Morley Safer, "60 MINUTES"

"If you are thinking about buying this book— don't. Buy several. You will want to share Lenell's story with as many friends as you possibly can."

—Dr. Dennis Kimbro, Co-author of Think And Grow Rich - A Black Choice

"Mr. Geter shows us that adversity is actually a challenge or an opportunity for us to better ourselves. As we face each hurdle we can either let it master us or we can master it."

—Armstrong Williams, The Graham Williams Group

"Mr. Geter, your book was very informative. It will be very useful resource and information piece for all who read it. Thanks for sharing it with me."

— Kimberly Aiken-Cockerham, Former Miss America

Overcome, Succeed and Prosper ... Continued

"The readers of this book will find universals in his strength of mind and in his focus on strong familial support and common sense. He believes that human beings must respect God and themselves to be able to focus on family, and personal development."

—Dr. Calvin D. Hutson, Chairman of The Department of Communications and Languages, South Carolina State University

"This book should serve as a beacon of hope for parents and our youth. You have so accurately outlined and stressed the five stages that one must acquire to become a successful person. It is my hope that parents will read and discuss in depth the important lessons that you have shared in this book."

—Geneva B. Finney, Former School Teacher

"Lenell Geter's story and book are important. They take us through the depths of despair, felt — at times — by all who seek to overcome stiff odds and life's twists and turns. More importantly, his book and life teach lessons that can help anyone recover from adversity and fulfill their dreams."

—Darryl L. Mobley, Family Digest Magazine

"Lenell Geter certainly has the experience to draw from when he takes the pen or podium. His message in Overcome, Succeed, and Prosper is based on first hand knowledge he gained the hard way. Factual, sincere, organized and well written this book is a guide for anyone who wants to be successful against any odds. I highly recommend it."

— Jim Harrison, Artist & owner of Jim Harrison Prints

"Overcome, Succeed and Prosper is a profound source of inspiration and motivation. Every family and household should possess this publication as a primary reference. This book is a great source of encouragement for families and those who are determined to succeed. It is a source of disappointment for those who seek excuses for their failure."

—Augustus Rodgers, Ph.D., ACSW, Director of National Black Family Summit

Overcome, Succeed and Prosper ... Continued

"At a time when family values seem to have gone the way of the last dinosaur, it is very refreshing to have the doomsday clock rewound, and we begin anew to look at how families can be. This book is a must reading for those of us who still believe that the family is the background of any society."

—Marva Collins, Marva Collins Preparatory School

"Very few people could have endured the Lenell Geter experience without becoming permanently embittered. His extraordinary ability to overcome such a harrowing nightmare is superceded only by his willingness to share his formula for living a successful and enriching life. This book is a must for anyone who needs reassurance that, despite adversity, we can Overcome, Succeed and Prosper."

—Dr. Leroy Davis, President of South Carolina State University

"Most importantly, and in spite of his lurid and painful experience, Lenell Geter lucidly enlightens us with his five tools for success for our physical, mental and spiritual landscapes of life..."

—Faye O. Hardy, Retired Principal and Adjunct Professor, Benedict College

"This is one of the most practical, self-development resources available today. This work delves deeply into the inner recesses of human nature. It is a veritable tool kit for self-actualization, character development, making appropriate choices, and life skills in general. It will serve as a guidepost for anyone pursuing his or her existential quests and seeking to live a richer and more rewarding life."

—Dr. Leonard A. McIntyre, Deputy State Superintendent Of South Carolina

"Viewed properly, problems which challenge your family, career and social life should be viewed as experiences needing an adversity specialist. This book and its five attitudes for success provide the encouragement, the knowledge and the tools for individuals to specialize in extracting adversity, self-doubt and negative attitudes from their lives, which are ingredients that give life to problems."

—Lenell Geter, Author and Inspirational Speaker

Another Book (workbook) by Lenell Geter

Building Youth Character With Confidence

(Title changed from "Building Youth Character through Self-development")

Publisher's Cataloging-in-Publication
(Provided by Quality Books, Inc.)

Geter, Lenell.
Overcome, succeed, and prosper : the 5 attitudes for success to enable individuals or families to lead successful lives / Lenell Geter.
—1st ed.
p. cm.
Includes bibliographical references and index.
Library of Congress Card Number: 00-190302
ISBN: 0-9678783-1-4

1. Self-actualization (Psychology) 2. Success.
3. Geter, Lenell I. Title.
BF637.S4G48 2000 158.1
QB100-295

Jacket Illustration and design by Leo Twiggs
Jacket layout by Pat Callahan

Printed in the United States

Published by The Marzinza Publishing Group

The Marzinza Publishing Group
A Division of Lenell Geter Enterprises
Post Office Box 24194
Columbia, SC 29224
http://www.lenellgeter.com

Dedication

Dedicated, with love, to my wife Marcia

and my daughters:

Marquita, Nzinga and Zakiya.

Acknowledgments

Overcome, Success and Prosper could not have become a reality if it had not been for God and the help of kind people.

To my mother, Ella Mae Willis, stepfather, James Willis, Sr., and other family members, the late L.C. Hickson and Rose Lee Hickson, E-Systems friends, KKDA radio family, and other supporters around the world for your invaluable assistance, prayers and support.

Many thanks to Dr. James Walker, a man of deep discernment, for inspiring me to develop the concept I call *psycho-cultivation*.

I am grateful for the teamwork of Dr. Harry Faggett and Dr. Clearance W. Murray, Donnette Martin and other students at South Carolina State University for performing preliminary work and research.

I appreciate the initial editing of the book by Pat R. Outlaw, Gwen Gilford Foushe, Harriet Jones- Hammond, and Tom Brown.

The following incredible persons were invaluable with their thoughtful input, advice, and technical support: Dr. Dean Patrick, Carol Waldo, Carl Dunn, Faye O. Hardy, Leo Twiggs, Vicki Phillips, K. Allen Campbell, Victoria (Vicki) L. Shearin, Cliff Hopkins, Pan Callahan, Roy Smith, Rosemary Glover, Donald Wood, James Solomon, Marcus A. Manos and Carleton Giles.

Cathy Greene, thank you very much for the beautiful poem.

I am grateful to Robert Williams for typesetting services.

A special thanks to Dr. Sanita Savage-Frazier for her advice and suggestions for the format of the book.

I am richly rewarded and deeply grateful to my editor, Dr. Calvin Hutson, for his willingness to assist and to take time from his busy profession to make final proofreading and editorial improvements to this book.

And finally, thank you leaders, mentors and friends for the testimonies and for the sources sited in the bibliography section.

Contents

Foreword

Lenell Geter's practical and commonsensical book *Overcome, Succeed, and Prosper* is a true "profile in courage" and determination in the face of almost insurmountable hardships. In 1982, he had just begun a career as an engineer in Greenville, Texas, when during his short stay he was mistakenly charged, convicted, and sentenced to life imprisonment for a crime he did not commit. He spent sixteen months in prison before his name was cleared of wrongdoing. CBS's "60 Minutes" did a key segment on his plight in 1984, and in February of 1987, CBS Television aired "Guilty of Innocence: The Lenell Geter Story," a major motion picture for television.

In his beautifully written account, there is an underlying message, which inspires, informs and encourages families and individuals to overcome their obstacles and to make personal changes in their lives by employing his system of "Five Attitudes for Success" and "Character Benchmark Lessons." This informative account of a real life situation speaks volumes about the inner strength and the indomitable human spirit. His is the story of a man who endures anguish and horror and lived to emerge a man of undying heroism and hope—a man who peered into the deepest regions of man's inhumanity to man and of his own soul and survived.

The message springs from his experiences and universal truths describing the attitudes necessary to overcome that Lenell Geter, a courageous young engineer, actually experienced and now practices. These attitudes for success helped him to recover from a horrific ordeal and are now enabling him to assist others to achieve their dreams despite adversity. Families will be inspired and encouraged by employing his structured system to learn helpful lessons about adversity, character, values and success.

In his moving narrative of overcoming adversity, Geter makes the negative disappear with his positive advice to generations of young people who will benefit from his beautiful and enlightened advice.

He believes that human beings must respect God and themselves to be able to focus on family, and personal development. This message is a structured plan, which can be tailored to any individual's dreams and goals.

Who will benefit from his beautiful and enlightened advice? Throughout the book, he admonishes young people, and he says to all readers to be ready for any obstacle in life. His horror story unfolds so dramatically positive until it serves to motivate and to educate young readers as well as more mature readers. In other words, Geter will make the negative disappear with his faith in God, his five attitudes for success and his Character Benchmark Lessons to generations of young people and families. He is a proud American who is eminently qualified to write such a book, because he is a living example of one who dared to say no to all obstacles and hopelessness.

-- Dr. Calvin Hutson

Preface

The greatest answer for failure is to develop a frame of mind that is based on succeeding despite adversity. The answer is here! The five attitudes for success will aid people in avoiding trouble, in overcoming adversity and in becoming successful citizens. Portions of this book are autobiographical, inspirational, philosophical, and spiritual—which will benefit individuals and families.

I have devised a five-step attitudinal approach which is designed to bring meaning to the lives of people. This approach provides an effective way to pass on virtues and to give structure to the lives of those who use it. It is my desire that those interested in people will find the merits of the five-attitudinal approach to be many-valued, multifaceted, and relative to larger social, philosophical and educational viewpoints. In addition, I have included *Character Benchmark Lessons* to engage readers in vital discussions on character challenges or adverse matters with which individuals, families or youths may be confront with in the future.

From the point of view of an adult who actually lived through a very negative and unwarranted experience as a young man, these lessons hopefully will be more meaningful to young people who are confronted with questions on goals leading to at-risk or contrary pathways to the right goals.

As with any book which attempts to explore complex concepts which are controversial, there will be individuals who will not concur with some of the concepts. This is understandable. However, the fact still remains that we must not lose sight of the necessity to provide direction for young people whose lives depend on positive guidance. In this connection, anyone who can show that his or her methods are entirely successful at reversing the problems of our youth can, and is, qualified to cast stones of criticism. Fortunately, my preparation for life was balanced enough to help me endure one of the most horrible experiences imaginable. My "Texas Nightmare" can only be described as an inhumane obstacle to anything which is considered civilized.

In 1982, I began living my "American dream." I had just begun what I considered a very lucrative career in Greenville, Texas, when I was confronted with the most devastating experience of my life. It was during my short stay in Greenville that I was mistakenly charged, convicted and sentenced to life imprisonment for a crime I did not commit. Before my name was cleared, I spent sixteen months in a Texas prison.

The story was broadcast on the CBS, NBC, and ABC Television networks. It was, also, published in the *Texas Monthly*, *Jet Magazine*, and numerous newspapers. I, also, appeared on CBS' *"60 Minutes,"* ABC television, *"NBC News Today," "Nightline,"* and other television programs. On November 14, 1987, CBS Television aired a major motion picture for television, *"Guilty of Innocence: The Lenell Geter Story,"* depicting the circumstances leading up to my mistaken identity, conviction, incarceration and eventual exoneration. These media entities and others had a tremendous impact on my life.

I am not a family counselor or an expert on human behavior. Most of my information or findings are empirical in nature, i.e., from observation and experience. Therefore, this book grows out of my infamous "Texas Nightmare," which caused me to seek answers to questions on succeeding despite adversity—how to promote one's life after pain, trouble and suffering. Immediately after I was vindicated, I began to reflect on spiritual truths, for answers about human motivation, in order to make some sense of what happened to me.

As an outgrowth of the "Texas Nightmare" and all that I was exposed to, I became interested in learning how some family members or individuals might refrain from living a life of crime. I knew something had to be done about the gross waste of human life and potential once I was vindicated. Having experienced life from my vantage point, I was left thinking; *I have got to do something!* This is what this book represents to me—a way to inspire and educate the public and a way to salvage the lives of our youth.

Fortunately, sixteen months of incarceration among people whose lives were headed in the wrong direction seemed to make me eminently qualified to offer advice to anyone with problems as a common denominator. Moreover, the ideas in this book have been tested in my own life. These ideas will help to improve the attitude and self-image of people. They will also give them a better perspective on the importance of education, a better understanding of setting goals, and the ability to make adversity their partner while climbing the mountain to the summit of success!

PART 1

Negotiating Problems by "Walking in My Experiential Moccasins"

Nothing Too Difficult

There is nothing too difficult
Where faith is involved.
No mountain too high,
No problem that can't be solved.

People all around you
With voices to be heard,
There is so much power
In a dynamic word.

Yet you must put forth effort
To accomplish your dreams.
An idea is just that
If you don't have a scheme.

You stand on your principles,
Believe in what you say
And you can break through barriers
Making way for a better day.

For in this world of trials
Someone must see the light,
Raise your head up high
And join in the fight.

— By Cathy Greene

CHAPTER 1

My Texas Nightmare

Overcoming Adversity

Before we can realize our dreams, the one thing we will all, at one time or another, confront is adversity. One's ability to stand on principles and succeed despite adversity will be a prerequisite for success. In short, overcoming adversity in our families or as individuals entails confronting challenges, taking control and becoming victorious by fulfilling dreams.

Our dreams are assisted by individuals who want to aid us in avoiding problems and overcoming negative habits. However, people will continue to experience adversity, but their problems in the Twenty-first Century will be atypical. Millions of families around the world are being challenged immensely by young peoples' lack of respect for authority, by their abuse of drugs, and by their acceptance of and participation in teen pregnancy, violence and crime. Some adults are being challenged with the rearing of these children, with working more than one job and with drug abuse in their lives. If these problems were to be extended into the future, it would be enough to keep us busy working on solutions for years.

In the Twenty-first Century, the prominence of the internet and the computer in the average home will make information readily available to children whose knowledge will be enhanced by it. Often, the information will not be congruent with the values of their parents. The knowledge received from television, radio, and computers will be helpful, but some of this information will guide children down the wrong value pathway. When the five attitudes for success are used to bring structure to a youngster's life, the youngster will be guided by a principal-pathway from an intervention perspective.

To defeat adversity, my personal tragedy as experienced in Texas inspired me to formulate the five attitudes for success to my system called *psycho-cultivation.* Other books which focus on success do not include adversity as an undergirding factor in their principles for success. Instead, most books acknowledge that there "is an equivalent benefit" in every adversity. What most people really want to know is how to use that adversity for their benefit. It is not enough to acknowledge to football players that they will face opposition in their bid to win the football game. The coach has to prepare the players by introducing strategies into their game-plan with opposition in mind. In my system, adversity is included as a part of success, because in real life it is a part of reality and should be considered and included as part of a stepping-stone to achievement.

Adversity is often called a barrier. Yet, it is much more. It is alive in our daily experiences. When adversity occurs, it brings with it an array of emotions. When it strikes, it sometimes makes us sad, disappointed and regretful. When it is there with us, its hidden advantage is, also, there. Adversity's presence is an individual's opportunity to succeed by moving on with his or her life. Without a good plan of action and the confidence to sustain it, most people will not take advantage of their opportunities. Anytime the moment to succeed is not seized, the adversity often remains in the form of pain and regret. Those persons who are courageous enough to seize the opportunity will become victorious in the presence of adversity.

I have had the opportunity to experience some challenging adversities in my life's journey. I learned, over time, how to cope with these adverse experiences. However, a few big challenges tested me. With help, I managed to win! My faith in God, assistance from family, friends and strangers helped me along the way.

Previously, I relied on the five attitudes which I had not formally structured at the time. Then, it was not a well-defined system, but reflection and experiences helped me to develop it later. As you read this book, you will be convinced to do something about circumstances in your life or in the lives of family members, or anyone who wants more control in life. You will come to believe that if you sit down around the kitchen table with your children or others and review this book, you will learn to remain strong in difficult times. I certainly needed to be strong because a family tragedy hit me close to home.

Perhaps, the one person, besides my mother who had the most influence on my earning a college education, was my oldest brother, John L. Geter. John L. was quiet, short in stature and slightly overweight. He was a self-employed painter by profession. John L. was known for encouraging the family. He and his wife, Frances Geter, had five children.

Late in January, 1980, I returned home to Denmark for the weekend to enjoy my family and relax for awhile. I was in the bathroom getting ready to return to South Carolina State University, which is located in Orangeburg, South Carolina. Mom, Ella Mae Willis, was in the kitchen, my sisters and two of my brothers were at home. John L's wife and children were there, also. James Willis Jr., my younger brother, was not present because he was on military duty out of the country.

The family was quietly talking in the living room when I heard a commotion in the front of the house. I was looking into the mirror one last time before going into the living room to join the rest of the family. All of a sudden, family members were screaming. I rushed from the bathroom to find my brother John L., who was sitting in the dining room, struggling to breathe.

My youngest brother Ricky Willis and I quickly moved him from the chair and onto the floor. John L. was having, as I learned later, a massive heart attack. Ricky and I started giving him mouth-to-mouth resuscitation and heart massage. Someone called the Denmark Emergency Squad and they soon arrived. John L. appeared to be alive when the paramedics arrived and they attempted to revive him. They were unsuccessful. John L. died.

I was hurt! I loved my brother. He is, now, forever, in my memory. I often think of John L. pursuing his dreams. I remember that he struggled many times and succeeded in the face of adversity. He lived his dream of owning a painting business. John L.

was never satisfied with working for someone else; he had to work for himself. When things got rough for me in college, I remembered John L's determination to realize his dream. His attitude was a model for me to follow—his dedication and strength inspired me. He and my mother gave me inspiration. Their strength and commitment motivated me to thirst for a college education.

Recruited To Work at E-Systems

After graduating from Denmark Technical College, I enrolled at South Carolina State University (SCSU) in the mechanical engineering technology program. During my senior year at South Carolina State University, several firms offered me employment opportunities. One of my greatest dreams was realized—to earn a college education. I sat down with my girlfriend Marcia one day in a Wendy's Restaurant to discuss job offers. We were impressed with the town of Greenville, Texas. The town of Greenville is comparable in population to Orangeburg, South Carolina. Greenville is nestled near the border of East Texas. In contrast with nearby cities in Texas, Greenville has an abundance of trees.

I was recruited for an engineering position at E-Systems in Greenville. Five other students from SCSU also accepted employment there. E-Systems is a major employer of over two thousand employees. I adjusted quickly and felt comfortable living in Greenville. In my spare time, my co-workers and I played tag football, softball, and participated in Bible classes.

I was excited about where my life was headed. Everything was falling into place. I was planning to get married to my college sweetheart on Christmas day, and I was working in the area in which I was trained. I worked hard during the week, but I always enjoyed going to the park on Sundays in Greenville to read, to reflect and to feed the ducks. The park was such a beautiful place to sit and relax. The water was peaceful and the trees green. Long before the crowds arrived at the park, its peacefulness was there to be enjoyed by the "early birds." On the weekends, I was often one of those early birds. People were picnicking and children were having fun playing. Lovers were holding hands, quietly talking, laughing and smiling. It was a place for bonding with lovers or family members. I love to see people in harmony with the beauty of nature as a backdrop. It was in these moments of reflection and quietude that I dreamed of marrying my fiancee, Marcia, and starting a family. In July of 1982, Marcia and I discussed wedding plans. I had planned to return to South Carolina around the last week in August to finalize arrangements for our wedding which was planned for December 25, 1982.

My Arrest

The wedding, however, was not to be. In August of 1982, a gunman robbed several restaurants, including a Kentucky Fried Chicken restaurant in the metropolitan area of Dallas and also in the city of Greenville, Texas. The Greenville Police Department sought information from the community concerning the robber of their local Kentucky Fried Chicken restaurant. They placed ads in the community newspaper requesting information and leads. According to news accounts, "An elderly woman became suspicious of a black man who drove a Volkswagen Beetle with out-of-state tags. The man sat in the park near her home at the lake reading and feeding the ducks." She responded to the Greenville Police Department public appeal by reporting her suspicions concerning a "colored man" who usually sat in the park near her home.

I enjoyed sitting in the park on the weekends for relaxation, reading and feeding the ducks. The elderly woman was referring to me. I had no knowledge of the crime or any crimes. Though the elderly woman's fears were unfounded and unwarranted, I discovered later that her suspicions were motivated by the environment in which she grew up. Her mistake cost me sixteen months of pain and irrevocably changed my life forever!

The elderly woman's call prompted Lt. Fortenberry, a Greenville Police detective, to request photos from my employer along with a criminal background check from my home state. Lt. Fortenberry learned that I had no previous criminal record.

An employee of E-Systems, who knew me from work, saw the culprit in the Kentucky Fried Chicken restaurant robbery in Greenville, Texas. During her interview with CBS *60 Minutes*, she was confident in her assertion that I was not the robber. The employees of that Kentucky Fried Chicken also eliminated me as a suspect after reviewing a photo lineup with my picture in it. However, Detective Lt. Fortenberry continued to disseminate my photos, along with false information concerning my character, to nearby police districts. When referring to me, police departments were told he is, "a bad character" and a suspect in crimes back in South Carolina. My apartment was under surveillance for two weeks prior to my arrest.

My dream of marrying Marcia was shattered on August 23, 1982. After coming home from work that afternoon, I was astonished to be stopped by two plainclothes detectives pointing guns at me. I was told by Lt. James Fortenberry who identified himself at the scene and stated, "We are responding to a warrant from the Dallas area for your arrest." Of course, I was thinking that there must have been a big mistake—that shortly it would be cleared up. Hopefully, the only thing I would be left with was this horrible and unfortunate experience.

The detectives searched me, as well as my car. In the car, I had a book bag containing a Hunt County library book. Both were confiscated. I was reviewing this book in preparation for a course I was planning to take at E-Systems. The detectives took me down to the Greenville Police Department and booked me. There was something demeaning and unfair about what was happening to me.

Being arrested, handcuffed, and jailed was such a debasing experience for me. In the Greenville Police Department, I was interrogated, photographed, ordered to strip, body-cavity searched and placed in a cell by myself. To get to the cell, I had to take a few steps down and a slight turn in order to enter the dimly-lit jail chambers which were seldom used. I could hear the noises of inmates who were housed above me. Obviously, they had discontinued using this area for lockup on a routine basis. It was difficult to believe that people would lead a life of crime, knowing that being arrested and jailed are possibilities.

Shortly afterward, my house-mate, Anthony Williams, was arrested, as well as another engineering colleague recruited from South Carolina. In the six months prior to my incarceration, I had come to know the good character of all five of the engineers recruited to work at E-Systems. They were all very intelligent, highly compensated and decent individuals. All of us were earning nearly $24,000 dollars a year in 1982. I was confident, because I knew that we were innocent and had no motive to commit any crimes.

Those Hated Police Interrogations

The next day, I was driven to the Garland Police Department in Garland, Texas. I was booked as I had been in Greenville, and placed in a cell, alone. During my stay in the Garland Police Department, I met Detective Pat Martinkus and Officer Dennis Wheatley. They interrogated me time and time again, and each time I asserted my innocence and felt that a horrible mistake had been made. I hated those interrogations! I told them that I was earning a good salary as an engineer and that I did not commit the robberies.

After Detective Martinkus and Officer Wheatley interrogated me, I was afraid. I could see that they did not believe me. I became fearful of those two because it appeared to me that I was being circumvented. I felt that they were not acting in good faith toward me. I began to lose trust in them. My belief was soon confirmed because of what was about to happen.

A few hours later, it seemed as if I were thrown to the wolves. I became part of a law enforcement "feeding frenzy," as law enforcement officers from several counties were invited to interrogate me. I told them that I knew nothing about the crimes or who had committed them. At every turn, I was being accused of crimes which I didn't commit and given an identity that could not possibly be me. It was a horrible and painful experience for me. I felt that if I were white, it would have been ridiculous for law enforcement to make this quantum leap in their thinking. They were mistaken, because I only wanted to pursue my "American dreams" and to enjoy my work as an engineer.

I was told during those interrogations, "If you do not confess to these crimes, you're going to be charged with the other unsolved crimes." The next morning, I was called before the magistrate, and he arraigned me on over a dozen crimes in the Dallas metropolitan area. This made me more paranoid, cynical and distrusting of the judicial system. I now thought that the system was against me. I was being told by inmates that law enforcement routinely put "snitches" (informants) in the jail to listen in on you and plot a strategy against you. I remained silent and did not discuss my case with anyone. I decided to limit my exposure to the inmate general population by staying in the cell, spending my time, for the most part, reading and writing.

I felt a weird kinship, with Kunta Kinte in the television movie, "Roots" as it relates to the unwarranted deprivation of his freedom. I felt as Kunta Kinte probably felt when he was captured—angry, betrayed, surprised, and perplexed. This was my first time being in jail and I was in a state of shock. No one was answering my critical questions, "Why was I a suspect and, how did I become a suspect?" It was shocking to learn the answers to these questions after my conviction and as late as my roommate Anthony's trial. A benign act such as sitting in the park caused an elderly woman's conditioned fears to surface. Her actions became a catalyst for an overzealous detective to regard me as a suspect in the Greenville Kentucky Fried Chicken robbery. Also, in the Garland Police Department, no one was giving me any details or answering my questions. It seemed that things were getting more complex. I gave Rick McCants, one of my engineering colleagues, permission to withdraw $1,000.00 dollars, my six months' savings, to retain an attorney. When my attorney, Carl Gaines, came to see me in Garland, he stopped law enforcement from interrogating me.

My Parents' Arrival in Texas

I called my mother, Ella Mae Willis, and informed her of my arrest. Mom and my stepfather, James Willis, Sr., left Denmark, South Carolina for Texas within a few days to assist and to confer with my retained attorney, Carl Gaines. My parents and Carl talked over the telephone, but it was not a productive call. There was a disagreement among them, resulting in Gaines' dismissal from the case. Mr. Gaines and my parents developed irreconcilable differences. My parents felt that Gaines should have cleared me by now. I realized that the process of justice does not work that swiftly. In the meantime, co-workers began making contacts and raising funds for my defense.

The court appointed Edwin Sigel as my attorney. Court appointed attorneys had the reputation in the jail as being "sell-outs" for the prosecutors. In the beginning of our relationship, Sigel was optimistic that I would be vindicated. He had the ability to make one comfortable with the assurance that he would deliver. In a number of his former cases, he delivered a favorable plea bargain for guilty clients who wanted reduced sentences.

His non-confrontational skills were good for a court appointed attorney seeking a plea bargain from the court, but not well-suited for the combative atmosphere of a courtroom trial attorney who is fighting to clear his client's name.

Sigel asked me about getting out on bail. I knew an arraignment of over ten charges in Garland would mean that prosecutors could interrupt my life, if they wanted to rearrest me, while I was out on bond. Some in law enforcement threatened me with possibly being rearrested on these false charges. What my interrogators failed to realize was that I had never robbed anyone and this was a case of mistaken identity. When it seemed to them that I was being difficult, they flexed their muscles and flaunted their ability to affix charges against me.

As a court appointed attorney, I did not think that Sigel would sincerely be interested in helping me get out on bond. I had in mind that I would replace Sigel shortly. My family members had already promised to help hire another attorney. Because I had given Mr. Gaines one thousand dollars for pretrial work, I did not have much money left. I viewed Sigel as a pawn, doing the will of the court system. At the time, he was to me my adversary. I did not have any faith in Sigel. I was willing to forego getting out on bond if it took using my money to hire another attorney. My main concern was that I wanted an attorney who would not be a "sell out"—an attorney to replace my former attorney, Carl Gaines. I considered getting out on bail, but I had fears.

I became distrustful of law enforcement officers because they would give little information to my defense team regarding my arrest and imprisonment. Yes, I thought getting out on bond would be a great idea. Conflicting fears caused me to believe that my last bit of money would be wasted in a futile attempt to gain temporary freedom. Because of the number of charges against me, I could be rearrested on any one of them. Thus, I would have to post bond again. I envisioned myself alone among inmates, one thousand miles from home with all of my money wasted on attorneys and bail bondsmen. I would then be defenseless.

I was emotionally and psychologically challenged by this arrest and imprisonment. This monstrosity of an experience was traumatic and debasing. The thought of reliving this nightmare was too cruel and unbearable for me. The fear that was instilled in me at gun point during my arrest experience was the worst nightmare of my life—everything about this process was horrible. I told Sigel that I planned to retain another attorney. I realized Sigel would earn money if he pleaded my case and he would get nothing if he won it. I was under the impression that the judicial system was designed to move people through the court process by plea-bargaining, thus getting a guilty plea which saves the county money. Notwithstanding other reasons, I did not trust him when he assured me that he would protect my rights and keep me from getting rearrested once I was out on bond. Under these conditions, it seemed to me that it would be counterproductive for court appointed lawyers to take a case to trial, because pleading a case was how they made a living.

Sigel came to see me a few times and on one of his visits he told me the prosecutor was willing to plea bargain with me for twenty years imprisonment if I were willing to plead guilty. I was outraged and lost respect for Sigel. I asked him to help clear me, I thought he believed in me. It was difficult to believe that my attorney felt I was guilty, because he would not have asked me to plead guilty under any circumstance! Later, I realized the prosecutors had given Sigel shoddy police information regarding my reputation as a law abiding citizen in South Carolina and Texas. However, I told him that I was innocent and was not going to enter a plea bargain. At that moment, I vowed to myself I was going to trial! I continued to assert my innocence, but no one within the judicial system seemed to be listening.

Transferred to the Dallas, Texas Jail

I was transferred to the Dallas County Detention System after a week's stay in Garland. There, I noticed that the officers placed different colored arm bands on inmates. Some had yellow and blue, but I had red. Immediately, I wanted to know what these designations meant. After learning about the red designation, I found out that I would be sent to the worst section in the whole jail system. I was horrified at the notion of being placed with violent criminals.

Detention officers began linking us together with shiny, heavy steel chains, which made walking cumbersome. About ten of us were loaded on a van that was used solely for transporting inmates to and from the court and back to jail. On the way to the old Dallas County Jail, I could see the "real world" from the window of the van—the world of freedom. I belonged there! From my new perspective, I had no idea that the world of a prisoner was coexisting with the world of free people in this manner. I was moving about in the same time and space as those who were free but hidden away in this new clandestine world. However, there it was, just outside the window—the world of freedom happening concurrently with my life as an inmate. The people driving by did not notice me in the van—they could not have noticed my pain. The public had conditioned the justice system to work —out of sight—out of mind.

The van was driven into a dimly lit garage opening in the side of a tall building, and the garage door made a squeaking sound as it quickly closed. The van came to a stop. We were in the old Dallas County Jail which is located adjacent to the Book Depository where President John F. Kennedy was assassinated.

It took a few moments for my eyes to adjust to the abrupt change in lighting. We were given instructions as to how we were to exit the van. I was led chained together with the others to a holding area. They called most of the other inmates' names before they called mine. I became concerned and thought to myself, are they going to take me somewhere and hurt me? No, this was not the case. I was called last because this was my first time in the facility, and it took some time to get my paperwork finished. My constant companion was fear and suspicion.

As I was escorted down the hall with a correctional officer, I observed strong, iron, vertical prison bars with horizontal spaces. The bars served as a barrier with a dual purpose which was to separate people and to retain them in cells. People were locked up in the prison cells like caged animals. There was one big exception—humans have the ability to know the consequences of their actions and can decide to live an honorable life, free from crime and free from prison. Animals cannot be expected to live up to our standards. However, they bore similarities in their restlessness as they paced the floor or with their arms hanging through the bars. It was the most horrible sight I had ever seen. I had become a part of the world I just described. I am certain a visitor's description would be similar. Doors started clanging behind me and the correctional officer as we moved deeper into the jail. The guard stopped and opened a cell door which opened into a space large enough for two or three people to fit. I was told to enter. He locked the door and another door opened into a large activity room. People were smoking cigarettes, shadow boxing, playing cards, body punching, showering, watching television, playing loud music and talking. I left that area and moved deeper toward the rear to find a vacant bed where I could settle down and observe the surroundings.

It took some time to learn how to survive in this new environment. Soon, I noticed my days turning into weeks. Being incarcerated was taking its toll on me physically and emotionally. My skin was drying up and cracking like a dry desert bed. The facility did not have proper moisture in the air. I hated not being able to go outside and breathe fresh air. I had to breathe the stuffy air that was often filled with the stench of other people's flatus, cigarette smoke and body odors.

Reaching My Limits

Incarceration was difficult. It was hard to remain positive because I realized that this was real, not a dream. I suppose that is why so many inmates smoked cigarettes and drank lots of coffee. On one particular day, my emotional strength seemed to dissolve and incarceration began taking its toll on me. I had been incarcerated for several weeks and things were not happening fast enough for me. Visits from my co-workers Rick McCants, Wendell Crom, or Charlie Hartford would boost my spirits and so would visits from my mother. When mom visited, I showed my strongest side because I did not want her to know how dangerous it was there and at times, how hopeless it really seemed.

The dangers of incarceration existed at all times. The environment was very stressful. A person did not know what was going to happen to him next. In this system you were told what to do. Your advice was not needed. The fear of the unknown was the source of one's apprehension. One did not know who might be plotting against him without his knowledge or without provocation.

On many occasions, when I telephoned Marcia, the positive conversations we had would tremendously brighten up my day. For those wonderful telephone visits, I will always be indebted to her parents, the late L.C. Hickson and Rosa Lee Hickson, for allowing me to talk to Marcia at a tremendous financial cost to them. Their telephone bills must have been astronomical. The Hicksons were not the only generous ones during this trying time. My parents and friends accepted collect calls, and used their money to assist. I realized it was expensive, but I had to make contact with people for support and those who believed in justice as I did.

The mentality of most of the inmates challenged my ability to maintain a positive attitude. A part of my problem was not being able to rid myself of their negative attitudes. On one occasion, I found myself in a serious predicament. The reality of the situation in which I found myself was stifling. I could not get access to a telephone to call anyone. My agitation and distress continued unabated into the weekend. On Saturday, I reached my human limit. The close and oppressive confinement, the smoke, the noise, the inmates' attitudes, and my being mistakenly incarcerated had culminated in an emotional reaction from me. I just could not take it any more. I blurted out, "Lord help me!" One second later, after the sound of those words became silent, I heard the sound of a spiritual song coming from Evangelist Wade and others in the hallway. It was to me a small miracle. From this time on, I knew that God answers prayers and that He was watching over me. I rushed over to the bars that separated me from them to listen, to talk and to be encouraged.

From this encounter with those people of God, I began to dig deeper into the scriptures of the Bible for answers. I wanted to see whether any saints experienced what I was experiencing. I found my answers as I read about Job and Joseph who also experienced difficult times and unjust situations in their lives. I was encouraged because after their tribulations, their station in life improved immensely. I claimed and believed all scriptures that pertained to my situation, believing that the scriptures' divine revelations would be duplicated in my life because I was a child of God. Through, I believed justice would prevail in my behalf, but if I based the substance of that belief on my current circumstances, it would have seemed futile.

The two things that always reminded me that I was not a free man were the thick cigarette smoke and prison bars. I wanted to get away from the bars and the smoke. It seemed that the prisoners smoked continuously. I could see a thin, misty looking cloud of smoke hovering in the living area at all times. It seemed to me after breathing so much of this smoke day in and day out that I had an inflexible scab lining in my lungs. It was very obvious when I ran in place or had access to an area large enough to run or exercise. After a few moments of exercising, I would end up bending down with my hands on my knees gasping for air.

Court Trial by Ambush

Several days later on a Monday, I was ordered to the inmate's transport van. We called this going "down-and-out." I was about to be transported, but I didn't know where. We were never told where we were going, but I knew it could only be a few places. I ended up at the courthouse and to my surprise my case had been set to go to trial that day—I was about to pick a jury. I petitioned the court and asked the judge to address my concerns. I was visibly upset about what was about to happen. Emotionally, I began to voice my concerns about attorney Sigel's lack of trial preparation and while doing so, my pent-up feelings emerged. I attempted to dismiss my court-appointed attorney. I thought Sigel was derelict in his duties for allowing the case to proceed when he knew he was not prepared. I had good reasons to be upset because Sigel had not talked to my alibis nor was he knowledgeable of the state's case. I was concerned that he would make the defense look like fools or liars. When it was time for my case to actually go to trial, I thought the circumstances would be different. The difference would be my parents hiring an attorney to replace Sigel. I knew my family had raised money for an attorney to try my case. My time ran out—without proper notice to take alternative action, I was about to proceed with a trial by ambush. The judge did not dismiss Sigel from the case because he said, "the court will determine whether you are properly represented."

Judge Herbert Line, a retired judge visiting from Texarkana, presided at my trial. When the trial started, the 12-member all white jury out numbered everyone else in the courtroom roughly two to one. I am including myself, Sigel, the visitors, prosecutors, court recorder and Judge Line. At the moment, this was the most important event of my life which was rapidly succumbing to uncontrollable circumstances and from my vantage point it seemed that few within the system were interested in this affair.

During the trial, the state's victims gave contradictory descriptions of the robber. When they were asked to identify the robber in the courtroom, I was the only African-American in the courtroom. I felt, given the same conditions, any African-American who sat in my seat that day with that jury would have been chosen. I knew I had never seen those people before.

Around the midterm of the trial after hearing the state's case, Sigel began to believe me. I also began to have more faith in him, which increased as he worked harder to clear me. To come this far in my thinking was for me a big leap because he tried to get me to plea bargain. The plea bargain request caused our relationship to breakdown. I definitely thought he was against me, so I did not trust him and barely cooperated. Inconsistencies in the victim's testimony, shoddy police work, and prosecutorial misconduct caused Sigel to change and believe I was innocent.

When the trial started, my witnesses were not aware and my family certainly did not know that my trial was in progress. It was ludicrous. I could not believe that this was happening to me. It was all so sudden; it was difficult to grasp. As the trial proceeded, the judge allowed someone to telephone my supervisor, Charlie Hartford, who was at E-Systems working. The call took my co-workers and everyone there by surprise. However, the engineers rushed down to the courtroom. Nine engineers testified on my behalf, and I testified as well. During my testimony, I told the court I was at work when the crime happened. I thought that my innocence was proven. However, the prosecutors introduced two unusual victims. The Judge allowed the prosecutors to make an unconscionable move. "Furthermore, in a controversial move, Judge Line allowed the jury to hear from the victims of two other robberies who said Geter was the culprit in those robberies. Geter remains charged but untried in those cases," according to an article in the *Dallas Times Herald*, of Tuesday, December 13, 1983. It is unusual for prosecutors to inject witnesses from two unrelated robberies into an on going trial by jury during the guilt or innocence phase of the case — this action is heavily prejudicial against the accused. Because of this move by the prosecutors, Sigel had little if any discovery information on these two unrelated robberies. That act by the prosecutors tilted the trial in their favor. The court did not allow us time to address this surprise as the trial was in progress nor were we granted a continuance in order to reconstruct those days and prepare a defense for them. This move amounted to securing my conviction at any cost!

Life Imprisonment—A Conviction at any Cost

In October of 1982, in the 265th Judicial District Court, ten working days after attorney Ed Sigel had been appointed to my case, my life changed forever! Although I thought Sigel's performance toward the end of the trial had gotten progressively better, the jury had judged me. I was convicted of aggravated robbery by a 12-member, all-white jury. I did not think it was possible for this to happen to an innocent person; therefore, I was in a state of shock when the word "guilty" rang in my ears. I was horrified, shocked and troubled! Minutes later, I still could not believe what I had just heard!

However, the damage was already done, Sigel's final effort at end of the trial did not make up for his lack of proper preparation and his lack of belief in me. I was emotionally unprepared for the gravity of the verdict—"Guilty!" The word "guilty" seemed to have come so easily from the mouth of Judge Line, judging from his stone-face look when he said it. What did those words come to mean? To me, the word "Guilty" is reserved for crimes stemming from factual circumstances, but I had committed no criminal offenses. In my heart, I knew I was innocent! I could stand on my principles knowing that I could look anyone in the eyes, because I was innocent! However, the word "guilty" meant I was being transformed from living my dreams as an engineer to living in a hostile and life-threatening prison world. I would be among dangerous people who had committed some of the most heinous crimes imaginable. As the bailiff took me away, I looked back and saw the empty, shocked and outraged look on the faces of my co-workers.

A couple of days later, I went before Judge Line for sentencing. At the sentencing phase of the trial, I sat in disbelief at the awful things that were said about me from law enforcement officers who I knew were lying about my character. I was powerless to do anything in my defense. I knew I was in good standing in any community in Texas and South Carolina. At the sentencing phase of the trial, some of those same law enforcement officers were asked about my reputation in the community. These comments were given: "It was bad;" "I would say it's bad"; or "bad." I was sentenced to life imprisonment! There was no physical evidence linking me to any crimes and no one was harmed.

All of my co-workers were there in the court room with me during the sentencing phrase. Just six months earlier I had met many of them for the first time. Yet, this day they stood there in the courtroom with me to validate that the administering of justice should be just and color blind. It was not just! The majority of my defense witnesses were white; some were black. They believed, just as I believed, in justice for all. In this connection, I often wonder to this day why the prosecutors and many of the law enforcement officers did not value the truth. Surely, they must have known that their case was wrong. Innuendoes and criminal labels, in general, were used to incite and to inflame the jurors' minds in order to get a conviction. Therefore, suggestive photo lineups were used to buttress their case.

During the trial, the prosecution team which consisted of Ken Carden and Randy Isenberg, made remarks about me that were not true. For example, I was referred to as a "Jekyll-and-Hyde" criminal and a "recreational robber." After I was released from prison, a local TV reporter told me that while having a conversation with a prosecutor from Wade's office he asked, "If Lenell is a Jekyll-and-Hyde and recreational robber type personality, then what are the chances that all five engineers have that same personality type since all of them were considered suspects at one time?" That was the last time that label was used. Fortunately, my case began to get widespread attention after a January 6, 1983 article appeared in the *Dallas Times Herald* which described the unjust circumstances surrounding the case.

Struggling, But Giving God the Glory

I started a Bible study class in the day-room of the prison and had several people in attendance on a regular basis. One day, I did not feel like having the Bible class. That evening I did not want to help anyone with reading or math. I was depressed; I needed some uplifting. I was still in shock over having been convicted for a crime that I did not commit. The realization of the sentence "Life in Prison" was becoming almost unbearable. My spirit was at an all-time low. In times like these, I developed the habit of finding something good or something in the environment to praise God for and give Him the glory. I began to give God the glory for my exoneration. I prayed and praised God that evening, believing that somehow He would answer my prayers. I transformed those statements into affirmations and bathed my mind with these thoughts.

I learned to understand the power of praising better from a book that I began to read in the Dallas Detention system. The book was called, *Prison to Praises*. It was a dynamic book! It taught me how to give glory to God by praising Him for handling the situation and working all things out for my good. When I ran out of personal reasons to praise God, I would praise Him for the beauty of nature. I did not want to give Satan any foothold because I had to believe that God would come to my aid. I had no other hope! I wanted to make sure that God was near. I made sure my thoughts were not malicious toward my enemies. I realized that God does not answer the prayers of those with malicious hearts. I wanted my prayers to reach the realm where God answers prayer. Consequently, I felt God would take care of my adversaries. Although I was in bondage, I believed the judicial system could not take away my God-given freedom of spirit. I could still exercise my freedom to enjoy God's freedom of spirit through faith and praise.

Texas Imprisonment at the Tennessee Colony

I learned from a visitor that George Hairston, the attorney from the NAACP, was coming to see me at the jail the following day. I was happy because I saw George as the answer to my dilemma. I needed an attorney that was free from the political and economical environment of Dallas in particular and Texas in general. I thought I might be compromised if a local attorney solely handled the case.

That night while laying on the top bunk-bed, I began to praise God. I said in a hushed voice, "Praise God for the Lord Jesus." I must have said this phrase to myself hundreds of time. In a dream that night, the setting was prison, and George Hairston was seated and I was standing. He said something that caused me to be encouraged. He made a statement and I said, "You mean I can go now!" I interpreted the dream to mean he would be the one to help win my freedom. Until then, I had never seen George before, but the image in my dream was similar to George's actual features.

That night, I heard my name called. Immediately, I realized that I was about to be transported to the Texas Department of Corrections. I knew I was being transported because they always transported inmates late at night for security reasons. I became cynical because they were transporting me on the eve of George's visit. I heard all of the horrible things about prison. Being awakened from sleep in the middle of night made my heart pound like a drum—I was afraid beyond reason! I felt betrayed by the Texas Judicial System. I became apprehensive because I was locked in a real life drama due to a breakdown in the justice system. While waiting to be transported, most of my time was being consumed waiting for legal documents and personal affects from the Dallas Detention system. These documents had to be processed before I could be transferred into the care and control of the Texas Department of Corrections.

I would learn later that personal control of my time and environment was no longer mine. I did not know what was going to happen to me from one moment to another. I was forced into the prison environment where brutality, debasement, confinement and rape were everyday facts of life. That night seemed too long! I passed the time napping on a concrete bench or sitting on the floor.

In preparation to be transported, the Texas correctional officers chained several of us together. The officers' uniforms were different from those that I had seen so far. They wore blue and gray uniforms, cowboy boots and hats. When we were released to the correctional officers, we then boarded a white bus. The windows had steel mesh wiring which was installed to keep the inmates from escaping. The bus was compartmentalized into three sections. Each officer was separated from us in his own area by a wall made of the same strong steel mesh wiring, as do the windows. The bus driver occupied the front compartment, an officer in the rear was armed with a shotgun and in the largest compartment, sat the inmates. The seats in the inmate's compartment were bleachers which were positioned so that the inmates faced each other. I thought, what if there were an accident or a fire, we would perish because we were chained to one another.

After roughly a month in the Diagnostic Unit of the Department of Corrections, I boarded a bus to be transported to one of several prisons in the state. The bus passed through the town of Palestine, Texas, early one morning. On the outskirts of town, the bus was beginning to approach what appeared to be a huge hospital-like complex in the distance. As the bus came closer, I realized that this was a super large prison. The building was shaped similar to the letter "X." The facility was a multi-storied, brick building with several wings. It was entirely fenced in with razor wiring which was designed to cut, mangle and tear the flesh down to the bone on contact. Situated along the rectangularly shaped circumference of the fence, and located in the far corners were guard towers at least three stories high. The correctional officers had rifles in the towers and they were trained to use them, if the need arose. When the bus reached the prison gate entrance, it came to a stop. The officers on the bus had to surrender their weapons at the gate. A rope with a cloth bag attached to it was lowered from the guard tower. They placed their weapons in the bag and the bag was pulled up into the guard tower.

There were about ten of us scheduled to get off at this stop. Our names were called and we were relieved of our constraints. We formed a line and were ordered to march toward the outer wing of the building and into a television day-room. After an hour's wait, we were instructed to move inward toward the warden's office which was near the church and the cafeteria, located near the geometric center of the complex. Along the way there were guys hollering at us. They were using obscene words and catcalls to frighten us and to suggest a desire for homosexual relationships.

We went in the warden's office, a little troubled, one at a time to talk with him. The warden informed me that there may come an occasion when I might have to fight. Because not only was this where they housed their toughest inmates, but also "I may have to fight to defend my manhood." The warden was not encouraging me to fight under any circumstances, but it seemed that this warning was part of his routine monologue to new inmates. I became concerned for my well-being!

I left the warden's office and began walking the long hallway leading toward the place where two wings merge. I was shown the living area, but I could not believe what I was seeing. On the first floor, there was a fenced-in area where clothes and toiletries were dispensed. While I was requesting clothes and work shoes, I looked up three stories. People were making noises and talking while their arms were dangling between the bars.

Again, these men were living as if they were caged animals. I got my clothes and went up a few flights of stairs and into the cell, the living space assigned to me. The space was about five feet wide and nine feet long. The bottom bed was already taken so I naturally took the top bed. The guy that occupied the cell was pleasant, although it was clear to me that he was not to be trusted. It seems that he had contempt for my college education because he would refer to me as "college boy," sarcastically. I was told by the fellow that the clothes and boots were to be washed in the commode. The sink was reserved for washing the face and hands. Everything was divided into halves. I had half of the sink top for my toothbrush and deodorant and he had his half.

A Typical Day in Prison

The call for breakfast came early. After working in the fields, I like to get something to eat because the work was hard. I put on my state issued white shirt, white trousers and boots. When the call came, I went down to the first floor and into the large cafeteria, which had the capacity to feed a thousand people. It had to be large because the inmate population was nearly two thousand. We were given a healthy portion to eat. The rule was eat what you were served.

I would go back into the cell after eating breakfast. The call came for my floor to go "down-and-out." We assembled downstairs for the correctional officers to inspect the groups. Various groups were called and were lined up one after the other. We stopped at the same gate where I had arrived not too long ago. Only the correctional officers went through the meshed door first. Their firearms were lowered down to the officers and they mounted their horses. When our group was called, we exited a small door next to the large entrance. On the other side of the gate awaiting us was a tractor which was attached to five flat wagons connected in series. We were situated back-to-back on the wagon.

At the work site were trees and brushes that were assigned to us to be cleared for a cow pasture. The work was hard and my shoulders bled because of the heavy logs we had to hoist. Yet the countryside was beautiful and naturally landscaped with small, gentle rolling hills. From a distance, I could see inmates dressed in their white outfits laboring in the small valleys and on the hills.

One day when I was working, an inmate started taunting me. I heard his oppressive words in the background about me, and I suddenly thought to myself, I'm not supposed to be here anyway, I stood up. When I stood up, he spurned on me and we exchanged blows. I realized quickly that this guy was used to fighting, because my blows almost never hit their target. I ended up with a fat, swollen lip from that exchange. I didn't know that just by standing up I was inviting him to fight. I should have ignored him and the altercation would never have happened that day. His attacks would have to take on a different approach.

We worked in the fields eight hours a day. On some days, we worked so hard I could barely stand. Some of the guys collapsed in the fields. The work was difficult and the long weeks away from my career, family, and fiancee were hard. I was always fearful and concerned for my well being. At times, I was depressed and angry. Yet, I never gave up hope because I placed my freedom and vindication in God's hands.

Each evening while returning to the prison yard from work, we lined up against the wall on the outside of the building and the call came to get undressed. When we reached the door near the shower area, we were required to submit to a body cavity search. I can understand the facility being located in a rural area and their concern for security, but the thought of completely undressing on the outside of a building in plain view of the public was debasing! This inhumane treatment went on for the entire six months that I worked in the fields of Coffield.

After the shower we received clean clothes. We formed a line and walked to the dining room to eat. The prison system conditioned me to eat fast, and I had grown accustomed to eating a plate of food in under five minutes. A correctional officer did not allow us much time to eat properly. We had to get finished and then get out of there. After eating, I went to the cell to rest, and read or play chess, or watch a bit of television in the day room. I was familiar with chess since Wendell Crom taught me the game prior to my incarceration. However, playing in prison helped me to improve. I played my best game of chess in the television room before retiring to the cell to read or write.

I decided to start-up my Bible classes at this location. We never had a large class but we had regulars. When I was alone, I would always open the Bible to Psalm 23 to read and to look at a small picture of Marcia as this is where I kept her picture. I would just gaze at the picture; it was the only connection I had with her now. If I felt up to it, I would write a letter to her. We weren't allowed to use the telephone here. However, we were able to use it when I was incarcerated in the Dallas County Detention Center. Exhausted from a hard day's work, some of the inmates would start conversations up and down the hall. The topic of most of the conversations concerned liaisons that were made with some of the gay men in the prison. After everyone was ordered into his cell and just before I would fall asleep, I became aware again that I was just a number there. The correctional officer would pass the cell with a clipboard and count the occupants of each cell. They counted me. This went on at every shift change and throughout the day.

Denied a Hearing for a New Trial

At my hearing for a new trial, Sigel worked harder to prove my innocence. The hearing was called so that my defense could petition Judge Line for a new trial based on new evidence which was not known to us at the time. This newly discovered evidence was concerning an inaccurate statement about my good character that Lt. Fortenberry testified to during my trial. My family was astounded and incensed when they heard Lt. Fortenberry's remarks about my character. My sisters, Annette Brown, Jennette Johnson and Clara Willis-Thomas, aunts, uncles, and cousins became united in support for me. They talked to people and kept me abreast by writing letters. Later, Mom did something she would not do under normal circumstances - talk to the media. My sister Rozia Burison and her husband Benny Burison, Sr. asked attorney Lee Bowers of Estill, South Carolina, to check into the source of the false testimony about me that Lt. Fortenberry made during my trial. While Lee Bowers assisted in legal work in Texas, he was my chief liaison in South Carolina.

According to a *Dallas Morning News* article, dated December 4, 1983, "Fortenberry testified that he had talked with Bamberg County, South Carolina Sheriff Ed Darnell, who said Geter had been a robbery suspect there. Darnell later traveled to Dallas and testified at a hearing on a request for a new trial that Fortenberry had misquoted him and that Geter had no police record nor had he ever been a suspect." In a motion for a new trial regarding Sheriff Ed Darnell's new evidence, Judge Line overruled it and I was forced to sit and wait on justice.

Involvement of the NAACP in the Case

It had been some time since Marcia wrote a letter to the National Association for the Advancement of Colored People (NAACP) asking them to intervene in my behalf. Shortly afterward, Dr. Oscar Butler, of South Carolina State College, as well as others, contacted the national office of the NAACP to encourage them to look into my case. The NAACP assigned Attorney George Hairston from New York to address my civil rights' violations as well as those of my roommate and others. I was fortunate to have George Hairston. It was as if he was heaven sent because I believed help had to come from outside Texas.

The NAACP was great at investigating cases and trying them with some of the best attorneys in the country. Over the years, the NAACP has helped open the doors of civil rights to thousands of African-Americans and others. I grew up having respect for the NAACP because of how it sought to level the human rights playing field.

Even though my situation was unjust, painful and unfair, it was an experience that I had to contend with. In prison, the solutions came when I handled problems using faith from my spiritual relationship with God. It was through prayer and claiming and believing the scriptures that I believe contact was made.

It was futile for me to seek an emotional solution. All of the crying and desires to fight and get revenge would not have helped my situation. And, yes I could intellectually articulate the problem well to attorneys and the media, but I felt my prayers would not solely be answered through the efforts of others. On the outside of prison, my family, friends, co-workers and attorneys were writing legal briefs, talking to the media, writing letters, and praying. I needed something more. I needed much, much more. I needed to know that I was connected with God through my relationship in prayer. This is what the spiritual-self is all about—anything which pertains to God and His relationship with us. I needed God's involvement through His blessings to bless the efforts of all of those people who were working in my behalf.

When I first met my lead attorney George Hairston, I immediately could tell that he would not "sell me out." Selling out describes a person who operates under the pretense of helping, but is really behind one's back carrying out his own self-serving interests. George was a deep thinker and strategist who believed in doing the right thing to achieve the desired outcome. He likes controlling events, yet he is content to sit in the background, if necessary, if that is in the best interest of his client.

George arrived just in time to save my co-worker, Anthony Williams, from an unfortunate outcome similar to the results I experienced at my trial. A key question had to be posed and answered in order to vindicate Anthony—a question for which the answer was not known in my trial. The question and the answer to that question, "How did Lenell and Anthony become suspects and why did we become suspects?" In order to obtain the answer to this question, George used the discovery process in Anthony's pretrial hearing to call the law enforcement officers as defense witnesses in order to get their testimonies. The strategy worked. We discovered pertinent facts to clear Anthony and to give the merits of my case prominence. His case led not only to winning our freedom, but, also, clearing our names.

My roommate Anthony Williams was tried and found not guilty by a jury in Dallas, Texas. I was so happy that he was cleared. This automatically shifted the attention to me and momentum increased to clear my name. I was in the building during Anthony's trial. I was not called to testify. Some of the E-Systems employees were not able to attend Anthony's trial, but Wayne Bennett's wife, June Bennett, was there every day religiously seeking information for the "Free Geter" defense team.

Those Powerful Egos

Now that Anthony was vindicated, George Hairston began laboring with the powerful egos of my attorneys in order to orchestrate their legal expertise to win my freedom. George withstood the emotional bruises, temper flare-ups and egos of my five attorneys: Joyner, Hill, Bowers, Hinds, and Sigel because he realized that they cared. In addition, George was the kind of person who always considered my feelings. He had my best interest at heart. He lived and worked in New York and would fly to Texas to see me as much as was required.

I needed divine intervention to empower my attorneys with the wisdom to successfully argue my case before the court. George utilized the diverse talents of all of my attorneys to get them to work in concert and to become a great defense team. Some of the attorneys were good with research, criminal defense, and others were good with the appeal process, getting things done through the court, civil rights and administration. At times, I did not understand or trust some of their thinking, but I slowly began to trust them.

During Anthony's trial, I was in a holding cell, with inmates with selfish motivations. If free, many of them would choose to continue their lives in a world of crime. Sitting on a hard bench in reflection, I began going over what was happening to me. I had begun an excellent career. My fiancee and I were engaged to be married. I was earning a good salary which enabled me to save money. It was only a few weeks before that Rick McCants, other engineers and I took part in Bible discussions during lunch at E-Systems. I enjoyed those times, and I continued Bible discussions in prison. I was living the American dream. Then, suddenly, an unjustifiable incarceration shattered my dream. Shoddy police work and lies were the foundation for my predicament. Yet, I knew I was innocent! I knew and believed, through faith, that I would be a free man again!

The *60 Minutes* Report

I believed ever since I was a little boy that prayer changes things. If this statement were to ever be truly confirmed in my life, this was the time, and if I ever needed God to answer my prayers, this was the time. I was able to cut the strings of this painful past by allowing my spiritual-self to dominate my life. A person's spiritual-self does not age, does not hurt, does not seek revenge; it seeks only to love, to serve and to have a relationship with God. So what I really believed I needed was to allow my spiritual-self to connect with God in prayer in order to get a spiritual solution. I prayed, meditated, believed, and assisted as much as I could in my legal defense. At first the answers to my prayers began to come very slowly. I kept the faith and very soon the miraculous occurred.

On August 16, 1983, I received the following Western Union Mailgram from Suzanne St. Pierre, Producer, at *60 Minutes* CBS News: "Dear Mr. Geter, *60 Minutes* [is] interested in exploring a possible story about you. Would like to meet with you to talk about your trial and sentence and possibility of filming with you at a later date with Morley Safer. Please write as soon as possible or phone collect at."

Morley Safer and his staff came to interview me at the Coffield Prison at Tennessee Colony, Texas. I was familiar with Morley Safer, because I had seen him on the television program called *60 Minutes*. He was a tough, no nonsense journalist; I had a lot of respect for him. However, I was happy to see him because I knew my case was a miscarriage of justice and I needed exposure. Morley seemed to be a man of about fifty years old. He had a clear and deep radio personality voice. My concern was whether I would be calm enough to tell my story. This was a once in a lifetime opportunity. After the interview was over and Morley and I were having a conversation, he heard something I said that interested him. We returned to the interview process and he asked me a question about the statement I referred to earlier. I stated that I was a "hostage," because I was innocent. Morley was interested in why I considered myself a "hostage" in the Texas Judicial System. I felt that I was a "hostage," because I was accosted without provocation and placed in a detention center against my will. The situation left me disoriented. The American dream was supposed to be available to anyone who did not break the law, who worked hard, and who was willing to contribute to society. I could not believe that this could be happening to me!

Before Morley came to see me, I had already spoken several

times to a young associate producer named Marti M. Galovic, who was assisting the producer, Suzanne St. Pierre, with research on the story. Before my encounter with *60 Minutes*, other media had also been helpful in making the public aware of my plight. The local newspapers in my home state of South Carolina as well as Texas, television stations and radio stations were tireless in their efforts to report the facts which caused this travesty of justice.

At the time, I viewed *60 Minutes* somewhat differently than other news sources. The other news sources were good in their markets, but unlike *60 Minutes*, they did not have a national market to tell my story. Moreover, I was impressed with the unique format of *60 Minutes*. To bring national attention to the senseless injustices to which I had been subjected, I believe, in my case, justice and truth could only prevail through national exposure. My case needed to be examined by those Americans whose sense of justice was not distorted.

My defense team was excited about the newly discovered evidence that we were able to uncover. Some of our evidence consisted of testimony from my co-workers, Danny Walker, who was out of the country during the trial, and Debra Cotton, who did not know her testimony was needed. Also, our defense team discovered additional evidence from a victim from the Taco Bell Restaurant crime in Garland, Texas and witnesses from a purse snatching crime in Greenville, Texas.

I am not aware that prosecutors or the law enforcement officers passed to our defense team these favorable testimonies. Had we known at the time of the trial the nature of these witnesses' testimonies, then the prosecution's case would have been proven totally false.

Because the media were interested in the facts of the case, their involvement became instrumental in exposing my injustices. Therefore, the best way to explain what *60 Minutes* achieved was that the program allowed for the bits and pieces of information and evidence to be put together, like the pieces of a puzzle. On television, viewers saw the story come together. This gave truth to the saying, "a picture is worth a thousand words."

On December 4, 1983, Morley Safer shocked viewers all over this nation as he reported on the circumstances surrounding my wrongful arrest and conviction. After the *60 Minutes* segment was aired, there was a tremendous amount of support across the country for me. In writing about the program in its December 13, 1983, edition, the *Dallas-Times Herald* reported, "A CBS spokeswoman said about 40 million viewers watched the news program, which prompted the largest number of letters in the show's history." The viewers were outraged after watching the *60 Minutes* segment. Many felt that I did not receive a fair trial. According to information in the Freedom of Information Act (FIOPA). President Ronald Reagan's office, and politicians were bombarded with telephone calls and letters in response to that report.

The *Dallas Morning News* on December 13, 1983 in its "Chronology of Legal Battles" reported, "Dec. 12, 1983 - Dist. Atty. Henry Wade says he will join (the) defense in seeking a new trial —or drop the charges if Geter passes a polygraph test." District Attorney Henry Wade apparently did not put much weight in the polygraph test I had previously taken. During a period when I was still incarcerated, this first polygraph was administered under less than ideal scientific circumstances. When the test was concluded, my attorneys and I were told that the results were inconclusive. Later, we heard I did not pass the test. Prior to the moment the test was given, I had no idea I was scheduled to take a polygraph. Because of the conditions under which the test was administered, my attorneys wanted another polygraph test given.

The polygraph examiner was not able to get me to relax. My attorneys had no control over the location or the conditions under which I was administered the test. The location and site of the examination were poor, as the room was cold, dimly lit, and barely larger than a closet. In addition, the polygraph examiner would not allow us to have the results of his polygraph test examined by an independent examiner.

On December 15, 1983, an article in *The Dallas Morning News* summed up the circumstances under which the polygraph was administered. Ed Sigel, who was present during the testing, made the following remarks to the newspaper reporter: "... they gave the test in a five-by-five sheriff's office. I mean, this place had no windows; it was in the basement; it was the place they used to beat up people..." The operator "came out and said the test was inconclusive," Sigel said. "He said he (Geter) showed some deception, but he didn't pass or fail." Shortly afterward, I passed two polygraph tests and was administered a truth serum test, utilizing drugs and hypnosis, which I also passed.

CHAPTER 2

Vindicated!
Free At Last!

The Countdown to Freedom

I was overjoyed to witness the first step toward my vindication which was assured to me by my prayers and faith several months before—my freedom! Judge Ovard from the 265th Judicial District Court agreed with the prosecutor to set bond so that I could be free on bail to prepare for my new trial. Ed Garrett, a manager at E-Systems, posted the $10,000 dollars bond needed for my release from his personal funds.

The media were at the Dallas County Lew Sterrett Justice Center to record my historical first walk back into freedom on that momentous day—December 15, 1983. A reporter at *The Dallas Morning News* described the scene this way: "After posting the bond, Geter's supervisor at E-Systems, Charlie Hartford, said he was glad that Geter would soon be released. 'It's the first step in proving he's innocent,' Hartford said, 'I feel elation.' About 15 minutes later, Geter walked through a set of electrical doors and into a waiting mob of reporters and camera person. Under the glare of about 30 television cameras and photographers' flashes, Geter, dressed in a navy pin-striped suit, white shirt and navy tie, walked slowly down a short hallway into the Sterrett Center to stage a news conference."

Later that evening, Wendell Crom and Charlie Hartford thought it would be a big surprise to attend the services of Clark

Street Christian Church in Greenville, Texas. The church was having a fund-raiser for me. So we rushed there to thank them for their support; however, they asked us to make a few comments. They were happy that we came. We had to be quick in our visit because I was scheduled to be on *Nightline* back in Dallas in a few hours. That night I was tired and wanted to sleep, but George Hairston and I appeared on CBS' *Nightline* with Ted Koppel.

I decided to return home to South Carolina for Christmas, and to my surprise, there were television cameramen on the airplane recording this moment in my life. When I exited the terminal, I received a hero's welcome from over 200 well wishers. The press conference was packed with a number of reporters from all over the country.

My girlfriend Marcia was waiting there for me, as pretty as ever, with roses in her arms, standing near my mother and other family members. Dr. Oscar Butler and Mrs. Daisy Johnson, accompanied by others from South Carolina State University, were also there.

My lead attorney, George Hairston, advised me to settle down first and regain a sense of normalcy at home in South Carolina before making a decision to accept District Attorney Henry Wade's offer to take a polygraph test and pass it before charges can be dismissed. George arranged two polygraphs to be administered to me, both of which I passed. The first polygraph was administered in South Carolina by Frank Faulk, a former chief polygraph examiner for the S.C. Law Enforcement Division. The second polygraph was administered in New York City by one of the best examiners there, Nat Laurendi of the Polygraph Analysis Center of New York. Also, as I mentioned earlier, I was administered a truth serum and I passed that test. I did not have to take a polygraph test to be administered by the prosecutors, because they found the guy who they believed committed the crimes for which I was charged and convicted.

Going Back to Texas

I had not made a concrete decision as to whether I wanted to live again in Texas. However, an unusual experience helped to shape my decision to go back. One day, I was at my parents' home during the Christmas holidays when something within my spirit said, "Go back to Texas!" It was not audible words, yet I noticed it twice. Looking at this another way, and in a secular sense it was like being able to notice your sixth sense. I paid no attention to it the first time, but the second time I knew what I was going to do. Returning to Texas became clear to me in that instant. From that moment on, I had no doubt whether I would go back to Texas. My family didn't want me to return. I thought if God protected me in prison, He could surely protect me in Greenville, Texas. Initially, I was hesitant about returning to Texas for fear that I would be harassed by some in law enforcement. This fear did not deter me. Nearly one month later, I returned to Greenville, Texas to live and resume my career at E-Systems. I would eventually live there for four years after my exoneration before returning to live in South Carolina again.

Uncovering a Miracle

Two investigators, Jim Humpreys and Kari Momsen, walked into my life and volunteered to do investigative work free of charge, something we really needed, although we weren't completely sure that they were sincere. I thought that maybe they were the opposition team's implants. I think George Hairston felt the same way. So, George tested them. He asked them to do something that I'm sure, if they weren't loyal, they would not have done. They turned out to be genuinely interested in my welfare. They learned of my plight from the media and felt that they could be of help.

Though Jim and Kari were helpful in many instances, it was during my hearing for a new trial that they were instrumental in finding an important witness for us. They uncovered a miracle for our defense team. My attorneys named this witness, "The Queen for a Day." During my trial, she was known to the law enforcement officials, but she was not known to the defense. She was a young victim whose testimony would have extricated me from the Taco Bell Restaurant crime in Garland, Texas had we known of her testimony.

"The Queen for a Day" was told by police officials that her testimony was not needed. In addition, had she been called upon to testify, her testimony would have impeached the testimony of the prosecutors' key witness, the second victim of the Taco Bell Restaurant crime. The prosecutors' key witness and "The Queen for a Day" were the only witnesses to the Taco Bell Restaurant robbery.

The jury's opinion about me was no longer objective because the prosecutors had introduced two unrelated robberies - the Taco Bell Restaurant robbery and the Greenville, Texas purse snatching robbery, during the guilt or innocence phase of the Kentucky Fried Chicken trial, the underlying case. These nonmaterial witnesses, to the underlying case were allowed to sit in the witness box and discuss their allegation against me in front of the jury. As has been stated previously, my attorney Edwin Sigel was unprepared to address the surprise introduction of these two cases. I realized I was thinking as a layman then, but I recalled sitting at the defense table thinking that the prosecutors were skillful in how they interjected these two cases, thereby gaining the advantage to effectively try me, under the "color of the law," on the underlying case and having the jury predisposed to the knowledge that there were two additional cases pending against me. Because of the way these two cases were utilized during my trial, they marked the turning point of the case in favor of the prosecutors.

This victim, "The Queen for a Day", saw the robber of the Taco Bell Restaurant but the culprit did not see her. She stooped down under a counter close enough to get a good look at him and close enough to touch him as he passed by. Jim and Attorney Lee Bowers wanted me to come with them when they questioned her. I was introduced as an attorney and sat there in front of the girl as they questioned her for several minutes. Her mother inquired about my name and at that moment my identity was revealed to them by Jim. When questioned whether I was the robber, she, emphatically, asserted that I was not the guy who robbed them.

My hearing for a new trial was markedly different this time. I did not have to leave a holding cell and to be escorted to the side-door to have my handcuffs and leg restraints removed by an officer. I did not enter the courtroom from a side door or rear door assisted by a bailiff. This time it was really different. When I entered the court, I entered through the front entrance. Because I was deprived of rudimentary acts of freedom, little things like this were becoming important to me. The courtroom was packed with people. The case had taken on the appearance of a high profile trial. I saw an artist drawing the courtroom drama and scene. However, cameras weren't allowed there. There were numerous reporters and cameras in the hallway. I was told a psychic was there, too— it was an usual trial!

As I looked in the crowd, I could not help but notice identical twins, seemingly in their early forties, dressed alike. They were sporting two small American flags in their hands. They approached me later and introduced themselves as Ina Daniel Mcgee and Nina Daniel Wheller, the Daniel's twins, "your supporters." The Daniel twins and a woman by the name of Vernia Coleman and I became friends. When I was married, they flew to South Carolina for my wedding.

At the hearing, we produced "The Queen for a Day" and it was obvious that the prosecutor's case was experiencing a setback. Their "spin doctor", a prosecutor, was trying to handle damage control. Her testimony was very effective and compelling. This hearing was the turning point of the case in my favor. During the Kentucky Fried Chicken trial, which was the underlying case, the prosecutors introduced a second "unrelated" case, a Greenville, Texas purse snatching crime. Unknown to the defense at the time of my trial, there were two witnesses to the case who saw the robber. These two witnesses saw the perpetrator and could have exonerated me from any culpability, but were also told by law enforcement that their testimony was not needed. It was *poetic justice* that the two cases that turned the tide against me during the Kentucky Fried Chicken trial were the same two cases that helped to vindicate me! When I think about these events, I am reminded of the scripture in Genesis which says, "But as for you, you meant evil against me; but God meant it unto good..." Genesis 50:20.

Case Dismissed: Cleared by the Victims

March 21, 1984 will always be an unforgettable day because Dallas District Attorney Henry Wade asked the judge to have charges dismissed against me after his investigators turned up a new suspect for the crime for which I was convicted. It seems that this new suspect told an informant in jail that he did the crimes for which I was charged and convicted. The five witnesses who identified me at trial viewed this new suspect in a live lineup. Four of the victims identified the suspect, while the fifth victim identified another person in the lineup.

Several days later, Dallas District Judge John Ovard dismissed all charges against me. My attorney, George Hairston, who was sitting next to me, beamed with joy for me when the judge made the ruling. This moment was the culmination of an experience to which no human being needs to be subjected. It bought closure to months of anxiety and uncertainty. The reality of the moment brought to an end a long legal and spiritual struggle for vindication and the restoration of my name. The following quote from the Book of Proverbs 22:1 is representative of the value I attach to clearing my name, "A good name is to be chosen rather than great riches, loving favor rather than silver and gold."

I was thinking, no more resting on cold concrete benches in jailhouses waiting for court to begin. No more taking orders as an inmate from others without my consent. No more cold sandwiches for lunch or sweet pastries and coffee for breakfast. No more living in a hostile environment and close confinement with inmates who care as much about a person as they care for yesterday's meal. I was ecstatic and grateful for my vindication which came as a result of the effort of many people who worked in concert to make my freedom a reality. Because of my belief, I was assured of my vindication by God through faith. However, approximately, two years later, I filed a civil suit and as a result of this action, some very strange events occurred. I will mention these strange occurrences later.

U.S. Department of Justice Concerns

After resuming my duties at E-Systems, I wanted to know what information was in my United States Department of Justice files. I requested all records and personal files from the United States Department of Justice through the Freedom of Information Privacy Acts (FIOPA). The FIOPA files contained U.S. Department of Justice and Federal Bureau of Investigations (FBI) memoranda and documents, newspaper articles and scores of citizens' support letters to President Ronald Reagan and others.

The memoranda and internal documents were correspondence used to inform and to update other departmental personnel of actions taken in my case. Non-governmental employees' names on the documents were blackened out to protect their privacy. The newspaper clippings were photocopies of an article pertaining to my case. The scores of letters from citizens' were from supportive people who viewed the *60 Minutes* segment about me and had written to President Reagan, to the Justice Department or to their congress persons for help.

An interesting document concerning *60 Minutes* was also among the documents. Linda K. Davis, a U.S. Department of Justice employee, asked a fellow employee Roger W. Hirsch, to identify the concerns raised on the *60 Minutes* segment and in the media. Replying to Davis in a memorandum dated January 16, 1984, Hirsch outlined his findings as follows:

"This is in response to your request that I review a transcript of the December 4 *"60 Minutes"* broadcast on Lennell [Lenell] Geter. I have reviewed that and the transcripts that I have received on other telecasts to identify the concerns of the media about Mr. Geter's situation. These are the concerns I have identified in the *60 Minutes* telecast:

1. Lennell [Lenell] Geter was an atypical defendant. He is educated, articulate, a good worker, had a good job, and had no prior police record.
2. He was a black man in a predominantly white community.
3. While he had no prior police record, the jury was told he was an outlaw by the prosecutors.
4. Many co-workers feel he is innocent.
5. His picture was circulated through a number of police departments in response to a questionable tip received by the police department from a white lady after running an ad vertisement for leads on an other robbery; in turn, the vic tims and witnesses in that robbery say Geter was not the robber.
6. The trial was "swift," in that the defense attorney learned on a Thursday that the trial would start Monday, and the attorney could not get a continuance.
7. The sentence (life) was very harsh.

8. One robbery victim selected his photo out of a second photo lineup, but not in the first one.
9. Geter was the only black man in court.
10. Geter's witnesses put him somewhere else during the rob bery.
11. Uncalled witnesses who could have put him somewhere else.
12. The eyewitnesses for the prosecution varied in their descrip tions.
13. There was no basis for the "bad reputation" testimony.
14. While Geter showed deception on one polygraph test, the examiner refuses to say he failed and will not re-lease the test to Geter's attorney for examination by another expert. Meanwhile, Geter passed tests utilizing drugs and hypnosis.

Other media telecasts have made these characterizations:
1. Geter was black and stood out in town.
2. Co-workers said he was at work.
3. Geter states the detectives probably coached witnesses on the photo lineups.
4. One commentator states that Geter's co-workers feel he was framed, a victim of racism.
5. Geter states the matter "is racially motivated on the part of a few."
6. Geter states he is innocent.

The Dallas County Prosecutor's office tried unsuccessfully to subpoena *60 Minutes* outtakes (research) on the story. In *The Dallas Morning News* dated December 13, 1983, Dallas County Prosecutor Henry Wade said, The television show was "slanted."

The FBI became involved according to a Freedom of Information Privacy Act document because of the following theory, "Our theory was based on possible perjured testimony of Lt. Fortenberry, which could lead to a possible violation of 18 U.S.C. 242. In the U.S. Department of Justice memorandum from Daniel F. Rinzel to William Bradford Reynolds dated December 21, 1983, a history of the case is cited as follows:

"HISTORY: According to a news article, Lennell [Lenell] Geter was convicted in October, 1982 for a robbery of a Kentucky Fried Chicken outlet in Greenville, Texas, and received a life sentence. A graduate of South Carolina State College in Orangeburg, South

Carolina, Geter was employed in a engineering position at E-Systems in Greenville. The February, 1983, news article in the *Charlotte (North Carolina) Observer* went into detail about the trial and noted conflicting testimony from witnesses, and an apparent conflict in the testimony and statements of Lt. James Fortenberry of Greenville, and Sheriff Ed Darnell of Denmark, South Carolina, concerning Geter's character and reputation."

"In a letter of complaint, a citizen sent the article to President Reagan and the matter was referred to the Department of Justice. Other citizens also wrote. Following a review of the article, we asked the FBI on September 28, 1983 to conduct a limited investigation, specifically, to obtain a transcript of the testimony of Lt. Fortenberry and of Sheriff Darnell, and to interview Lt. Fortenberry. Our theory was based on possible perjured testimony of Lt. Fortenberry. The results of the FBI's investigation were received by us on December 6, 1983."

The U.S. Department of Justice's conclusions and findings: "Conclusion: There is insufficient evidence to justify prosecution in this matter. The record is replete with possibilities of misunderstandings, miscommunications and lapses of memory. The disagreements between Darnell and Fortenberry may never be resolved; they certainly cannot now be resolved in favor of a prosecution for federal criminal civil rights violations on the part of Lt. Fortenberry. However, we plan to keep the matter open at this time and monitor any further developments."

Strange Events

After returning to live and to work in Greenville, Texas, three unusual incidents happened to me. All three incidents occurred after I was vindicated. The first incident occurred when a television station in the Dallas metropolitan area wanted me to appear on its evening news program. I agreed to do it. They sent a helicopter to pick me up. The helicopter landed in a field adjacent to the apartment where I lived. I had never ridden in a helicopter and I thought that it would be fun. Being picked up in a helicopter was to me flamboyant, yet I looked forward to the ride. It was a fun ride as we traveled along the interstate heading toward the Dallas Metropolitan area. The helicopter landed near the television station. I met the producer of the program. The live interview was brief and well worth the time and effort.

My case was still present in the minds of people. The amazing part of the day was when we learned that a reporter was hired solely to follow me for the whole day. When I left the station, I went with the station producer in one of its cars headed for Dallas. Behind us was the reporter who was now following us on the interstate. We could not "shake" the guy.

The producer telephoned the station to explain the situation and to request that an identical car join us so as to act as a decoy. The decoy drove up beside us speeding along with us 65 to 70 miles an hour. We had one advantage on the reporter. We could communicate car to car. We sped up a little and the reporter, who was still behind us, sped up also. We darted in and out of traffic in an attempt to confuse the reporter. The strategy was to confuse the reporter so that we could exit and let the reporter continue to follow the decoy. We confused him for a moment, just enough for him to miss us as we exited off the interstate. Thinking all of this was hilarious, I chuckled as the reporter passed above, still following the decoy, not realizing that we had shaken him.

The next interesting incident occurred one evening when I was looking for something in the guest room closet of our apartment. I was rumbling through the closet and noticed something dangling from one of my wife's large nursing books. I picked the book up and noticed a cord dangling with what appeared to be a receptacle on it. It appeared that it was designed to connect to another device. I opened the book and discovered wiring was tucked inside the book. I called George Hairston, after I had discussed it with Marcia to see if she had noticed it. He asked me not to bother it until he and the other attorneys had a chance to look at it. They had it examined and discovered that it was a low tech "bug," a listening device, used to listen in on our conversations.

It seemed that somehow someone had gotten into our apartment and hooked up a tape recorder to this device. We flew in one of the top experts from California in the field of surveillance and counter surveillance to electronically "sweep" my apartment for additional bugs. He brought in his sophisticated electronic equipment and swept the apartment but found no other bugs.

On another occasion, one Sunday when my wife, daughter and I were on our way to church, we noticed a van circling the apartment. I was the first to take notice because I was closer to the car than my family. The van was rust in color. It had two windows in the back doors, and no windows on the sides. I said to Marcia, as the van passed us, "I saw this van pass just before you got out here and the driver was looking in our direction." We quickly got into our car and I noticed the van following. We took a right turn out of the apartment and he took a left turn. However, in my rear view mirror, I noticed that he hurriedly turned around in the road and was following us again. So I turned around in the road and he passed us. We darted off toward town, and I noticed that he had stopped following.

Later, I felt that this incident was probably related to the investigative work being done by one or more of the litigants in my civil action lawsuit. This lawsuit was eventually settled, and I received a settlement amounting to nearly a year's salary. It was a small victory for me, but it was the principle behind this whole ordeal which led me to take legal action.

The Movie,
"Guilty of Innocence: The Lenell Geter Story"

In 1986, I met with several television producers who wanted to produce a made-for-television movie about my life and experiences. My attorney, George Hairston, and I were flown to Hollywood to see one of the producer's operations. Later, we were flown to New York City to meet with another producer from Embassy Television. Still another producer gave a big reception for me at the Leows Anatoles Hotel in Dallas, Texas. He rented a chauffeured stretch limousine to take me back to my apartment in Greenville, Texas. I was impressed!

They all were great, but I chose Norman Lear's Embassy Television Company to produce the movie. I knew personnel at Embassy Television had the ability and the experience to produce a quality picture. Embassy Television sent Television script writer, Harold Gast, to interview Marcia and me and to get our story. Harold, a veteran writer, was probably 60 years of age. He had a northern accent and reminded me of a casually dressed retiree who was more apt to be found in Florida with his wife.

Our co-producer made arrangements for Marcia and me to meet the actor and actress who were going to portray us. Dorian Harewood was chosen to portray me and Debbie Morgan was chosen to portray my wife. Dorian and I met in his hotel room where we sat and talked. Dorian was a pleasant and a polite guy who was personable. He was slightly shorter than I but had a booming voice. I believe if he were not a successful movie star, he would be thriving in another endeavor. Like me, Dorian enjoyed playing basketball. I had no idea that he was studying my expressions and demeanor and he was able to portray me easily.

Marcia and Debbie were alone and she was also studying and asking questions of my wife. Debbie was an attractive woman, with a gentle and friendly personality. We met other cast members including Paul Winfield, Hoyt Aston, Dabney Coleman and other performers and staff members. When the script went to production, I was excited. I was fortunate to be able to watch the actors and actresses being filmed for CBS Television movie titled, *Guilty of Innocence: The Lenell Geter Story*. The whole thing just seemed so unreal. Marcia, Marquita and I went to the set to view the filming of our wedding scene. It was exciting to see them portray us.

My major disappointment concerning the movie *Guilty of Innocence: The Lenell Geter Story* was that my mother and stepfathers and their contributions were not portrayed by characters during the movie. Their contributions were extremely important to me. Because, I did not realize that I was being tried so suddenly, my parents were not at trial. My parents went to Texas several times to see me while I was incarcerated and to attend to my affairs. In addition, they raised funds for my support and talked to reporters. They mailed money to me, wrote letters, took a loan out to assist me and they incurred many expensive long distance telephone calls. They recruited attorney Lee Bowers of South Carolina who helped to clarify conflicting testimony between Lt. James Fortenberry of Greenville, Texas and Sheriff Ed Darnell of Denmark, South Carolina. Most of all, however, they comforted, loved and gave me encouragement and support. Since my parents' contributions were not portrayed on the screen, I thought it might be perceived by viewers that they showed indifference and disinterest in my welfare. Of course, this is to the contrary because my parents were very much involved, active and interested in my welfare. I was the focus of their attention during this very trying time in my life.

When the movie was completed, I helped promote it by granting telephone interviews with newspaper critics in major cities across the country. A promotional company arranged the telephone interviews to take place in the comfort of my home. Nearly every half hour, starting at nine that morning to six o'clock that evening, I was promoting the movie. The promotion was effective and the next day millions of people read the articles and were interested in viewing the movie that evening. Marcia and I were flown to Washington D.C. to view the screening of the movie. The screening was sponsored by Embassy Television and cosponsored by the NAACP.

The Washington Post Interview

While I was in Washington D.C. for the screening of my television movie, *Guilty of Innocence: The Lenell Geter Story*, I consented to an interview with James McBride, a talented reporter for The Washington Post. My older daughter was with us. It was snowing lightly that day. My daughter Marquita Geter, began to experience playing in the snow for the first time. Reading the article James McBride wrote later, I realized he was very descriptive when he reported my daughter's snow playing experience.

Unknown to McBride and walking with us that evening was my biological father, whom I introduced by name only, not revealing our relationship. My biological father's last name is not Geter, so James would not have readily made a connection between us. My father was with us for the screening of the movie. To me, the meeting between my father and me was the real story because we hadn't seen each other for over two decades. Prior to this Washington visit, many years had passed since I last saw my father. He visited me when I was approximately six years old. Since my youth, my father has become a highly respected entrepreneur in his community and an active member in his church.

Because I was ambivalent about the meeting with my father, I did not want to reveal the reunion with him to McBride. My emotions were still too close to the surface. This was not the time, and I was not ready to address questions concerning our relationship. It was a strange feeling being there with my father who had abandoned me many years ago. I did not really know him, but I wanted to know him better.

Guilty of Innocence: The Lenell Geter Story was a major motion picture for television. My character, Dorian Harewood, was the main subject of the movie and I was depicted pursuing a career as an engineer in Greenville, Texas, when I was wrongfully convicted and accused of crimes I did not commit. I was living my career dreams in Texas until the travesty of justice occurred. After a lot of divine help and assistance from so many wonderful people around the world, the story had a happy ending. I married Marcia, my college sweetheart on June 30, 1984. I continued my career at E-Systems for four additional years before relocating to South Carolina. My experiences were so unusual and so great that most people will never be able to relate to them. Struggles usually precede victory; however, victory makes struggles worthwhile in the end.

Living in South Carolina Again

In August of 1988, my career took a change of direction. I resigned from E-Systems and returned to South Carolina with my wife and two daughters, Marquita and Nzinga. My youngest daughter, Zakiya, was not yet born. Among other reasons, my family and I realized we were stalling and living in limbo. Marcia and I could not bring ourselves to purchase anything that made it seem as if we were going to live in Texas, permanently.

After my vindication, I did not receive an apology from any municipality involved in my case for the irresponsible actions by their personnel. If I had gotten an apology from the state of Texas or compensation for what my family and I had to endure, it would have been easier to bear. None of the officials in the places where mistakes were made in my case were humane enough to come forward and apologize—admit that they were wrong. Consequently, I no longer felt that I could continue to live in Greenville, Texas. I had to think about what was good for my family. Greenville had ceased to be the place where we wanted to live and to raise a family. However, we had friends there and still thought of Greenville as a nice place. Nevertheless, we could not bring ourselves to purchase what we badly wanted, a home! We had the money to purchase a home, we came face to face with all the bad memories, we had to move on! My love affair with living in Texas was over!

CHARACTER BENCHMARK: LESSON # 1

Learning from My Struggles and Victories

As I vicariously examine my struggles and victories during my "Texas Nightmare," in chapter 1 and chapter 2, look closely at my adversity to learn what enabled me to hold on to my virtues and to my beliefs - discover how you can do the same.

The following five attitudes for success for overcoming adversity helped me to succeed; a purpose to serve others, a vision, a desire for improvement, an ability to overcome adversity and a productive attitude.

If people are experiencing problems in their lives or notice them in a youth's life, they can easily target those obstacles for improvement. Use my "Texas Nightmare" as a problem-solving model for hope and methodology for challenges as well as using the five attitudes for success to improve life. Use introspection to find the answers to the following:

- Our purpose is to serve others and to provide skills and talents. How do you plan to serve others or to provide skills and talents?
- Learn how to become motivated by a vision. What is your vision or the things that you want to acquire in life or do for others?
- Learn how to make improvements in all areas of life. What can you do today or what can you plan to do to improve your knowledge, education, relationships or spirituality?
- Learn how to realize and accept that adversities are experiences on the road to success and achievement. How are you going to utilize possible benefits from adversity and execute your strategy for overcoming?
- Learn how to align your labor as a productive person with your true purpose to serve and to provide your skills, experience or talents. What actions are you taking to improve your productivity—to be a better student, spouse, employee, citizen or person?

Forging a Brighter Future by Developing a Positive Attitude

It was my personal experience living among inmates that caused me to realize that these young people, in general, were suffering from a lack of purpose, belief and efficacy to lawfully manifest their dreams. The inmates did not act based on the premise that their purpose in life is to serve and not to destroy or take. I observed that they lacked some of the following attitudes to work successfully and to work actively from the core of their motivation: a positive purpose to serve others, a vision, a willingness to grow and improve, the ability to overcome barriers and the desire to maintain a productive attitude. In my studies, I have found that these five attitudes to overcome adversity exist in every successful person or in every venture.

The inmates faltered at the first stage—the purpose stage. They did not have as their purpose the desire to serve others. Invariably, their purpose when they entered prison was a selfish one: a determination to exploit others. Therefore, one of my main goals is to get people to realize that to lead a successful life, all of their undertakings should be done with the purpose of serving others and giving of their talents. I understand these concepts so well that I have coined the term *psycho-cultivation* to define the five attitudes for success to overcome adversity as outlined in my system.

During my imprisonment in the Texas Judicial System, I was able to view the untapped and enormous potential of the young prisoners. Most of the inmates were surprisingly young. I was devastated by this realization for I had pictured prisoners as being much older than the ones I found there. I knew these young men were from all across America—rural areas, small towns, small cities and large ones.

Naturally, a problem of this magnitude leaves one puzzled as to how to begin the process of change. After much soul searching, I decided to share my incarceration experiences in Texas using this tool so that individuals, parents and youth supporters across the nation can use this book to help with problems.

If a person were lost in the forest and I knew how to get out, it would be to his or her best interest to allow me to be their guide.

I call this method walking in my "experiential moccasins," because I am acting as an experienced guide. It is experience that allows people to help others! To discover how to succeed despite adversity, walk in my "experiential moccasins" and incorporate my five attitudes for overcoming adversity.

In the prelude to Part Two through Part Six of this book, the different stages of a plant's growth and development are used to illustrate the five attitudes of my system called psycho-cultivation. I chose the tomato plant as an illustration because it was familiar to me from my early childhood. I could have also used insects or animals as illustrations because everything has a purpose which is to serve, whether we realize that purpose or not.

The following are the five attitudes for success to overcome adversity of my system:

Attitude No. (1) Acquire a Purpose to Serve Others;
Attitude No. (2) Activate Your Vision with Desire and Motivation;
Attitude No. (3) Create the Foundation of Prosperity through Personal Growth;
Attitude No. (4) Use Adversity as the Building Block of Success; and
Attitude No. (5) Fulfill Dreams through Benevolent Productivity.

All life in the universe serves a purpose. However, through the ability to reason, human beings have the capacity to serve a higher purpose.

Each of the five attitudes for success and the fourteen character benchmark lessons in this book should be put into practice through personal use or under the guidance of a parent or a youth supporter who is involved in the training of youth. The five attitudes are formulated to encourage people to live a virtuous life as expressed in using the format in psycho-cultivation. The key is to get people to focus their energy into the right direction. The ideas in each of the five attitudes should be cultivated into our lives. Adults should take every opportunity to reinforce the five attitudes, especially with youth.

We know what we want the outcome to be when family members go through adversity. What people are not always clear on is how to teach children character and values under the umbrella of a structured format. *To understand* my system, called psycho-cultivation, is to study my infamous "Texas Nightmare," to perform the activities and character benchmark lessons, and to employ the five attitudes for success to help with overcoming adversity.

CHAPTER 3

Psycho-cultivation: Going Beyond Psychological Confinements

Freedom from Psychological Confinement

A prison is a place where society confines those who commit crimes against the state. By keeping these individuals confined, society aims to keep the general public safe and at the same time, rehabilitate the lawbreakers. In some cases, society has been successful with this approach and has been able to rehabilitate some people. On the other hand, prison, in some instances, has only been effective in housing criminals. However, for those who are only being housed, the behavior that landed them in prison does not change. While they were free, they associated with those who committed crimes and while they were imprisoned, they were among the same type of people. The inmates' behavior and unwillingness to change support this saying, "association brings on assimilation," which impedes rehabilitation. In this case, it is a negative association, because they do not get help to correct their behavior.

The prison environment remains a breeding ground infested with those who do not want to change. Prison has almost become a homogeneous environment of people who need to change, badly, but are not willing to change. The environment is nearly saturated with people having negative societal attitudes, which make it difficult for them to change.

On the positive side, there are those inmates who have worked hard to change but at the end of their sentences, after they have paid their debt to society, are left in a dilemma. Their dilemma was brought to my attention during one of my speeches to a group of highly motivated long-term offenders. These inmates were serving sentences in excess of ten years and yet they were not having behavior problems. They were either graduates of high school or in the process of earning their G.E.D. Basically, these rehabilitated inmates' major concern was that there is insufficient work-related infrastructure to support them after they are paroled. The solution to this situation is not difficult to solve. Society needs to make sure that these long-termers have a place to carry out the work release aspect of their rehabilitation once they are paroled. There are possibly scores of businesses which are willing to employ them. Also, they need to be able to amass enough savings so when they are returned to society, the money will be there to help them pay obligations, pay retribution, and support their families.

When inmates are willing to change, the prison system should be there to address their desire for change. Often the personnel in the prison system do not know how to address their desire for change because they cannot transcend the act of housing inmates. They need to be able to perform a needs analysis to ascertain an inmate's individual remedy in order to meet his personal need for rehabilitation. Helping the inmates to meet their needs by rebuilding their misguided values and principles moves the penal system from housing inmates to rehabilitating inmates. If their misguided deeds go untreated, then conflict will continue between the inmates and the society. Notwithstanding reasons mentioned, the inmates share the greatest blame for their reform. Every illegal deed which lands an individual into prison happens because the individual has a spiritual or moral problem which is in need of reform.

I want to make a shift from addressing the prisoner to addressing the average person who is stalling in life due to psychological confinement to comfort zones. I have noticed people having struggles in their marriages, their careers, their health, their social life, and their spiritual life. There are many reasons people become psychologically confined to a mediocre life. It could be fear, a negative self-image, poor self-worth, low self-esteem or some other psychological "progress inhibitor." Some people are able to visualize their dreams but are paralyzed because of their self-imposed psychological confinement. They are unable to progress because of their psychological bars which often appear in the form of fear which impedes their progress.

Psychological confinements (adversities, fears) are mental progress inhibitors which exist in the minds of individuals who are being inhibited from progressing, improving or realizing their dreams. They have decided that the comfort zone they are living in is safe. Making the necessary changes to move out of their self-imposed confinement creates too much stress. When they attempt to change, they become fearful of the unknown. Their willpower is strong, but their imagination is much stronger. Consequently, no action will take place because the fear that their imagination produces is stronger than their will to take action on their dreams and goals. This situation is alluded to in Paul G. Thomas' book, *Advanced Psycho Cybernetics*, which makes reference to Coués' Law as devised by Emile Coué. "The law states that when the willpower and imagination are in disagreement, the imagination will be stronger, and will cause the willpower to succumb."

The solution is for individuals in society to decide to pursue a dream which is greater than their fear and to overcome their psychological comfort zone in the process. They have to decide that goals and dreams are desired more than the comfort of staying behind the false and safe psychological realities of negative thinking. There have to be moments in their lives when they must be willing to decide to depart at will, act on their decisions and live life free from the confinement of doubt, self-imposed fear, lack of confidence and negative thinking. *Psycho-cultivation* is a powerful new concept that addresses this problem by utilizing the five attitudes for success, character benchmark lessons, faith in God, affirmations, rebuking negative thought pictures, living by mottoes and positive thinking.

The Origin of Psycho-cultivation

Looking back to the past, on granddaddy's farm, I realized the answer to the proverbial questions, "What is purpose? What are human beings placed on earth to do?" I thought that if I could find the answer to these questions I could make sense of my

"Texas Nightmare." This terrible experience was the biggest misfortune in my life! I became perplexed and started seeking answers to several questions. However, the answer was with me all of these years, yet I did not realize it. But while trying to understand purpose, I indirectly discovered a new concept that led me to grasp the meaning of purpose.

The answer could partially be found in the often contradictory dealings with human beings. However, the answer was not clear. Trying to grasp the meaning of purpose by dealing with this dichotomy is like trying to see clearly through a thick fog. When you study people, you realize the pain, violence and death they inflict on each other. People have not fully learned their purpose and the lessons that life teaches. One of these lessons is that people make choices and these choices can lead to situations that bless them or hurt them. The decision to choose is left up to them.

More times than not, you'll see a beacon of hope that is expressed through love. It can be seen when you care for your children or look after their well-being. It can be seen when you are stranded on the highway and a stranger unselfishly helps get your family going. Or it can be seen when a person starts a business that benefits the lives of others.

When I started studying the concept of purpose and the secret processes that led to the successful fulfillment of one's purpose, it took me years to receive the answer. I realized that I had talents and skills but I wanted to know what was my purpose in life? I conscientiously began to read intensely with the thought of discovering the answer to this question. I read nearly a hundred books before the answer came to me. I took notes, read, listened to people on the subject, and studied religious material for years. Though the answer finally came, and these resources contributed, I did not get the understanding solely from these sources.

The total picture came to me when I had a discussion with a friend, Dr. James Walker, a philosopher, concerning a proposal I was preparing. He used a concept that I was very familiar with but had not heard used in psychological terms before. He said, "They have to learn to cultivate their minds... with these ideas in their thinking." It was a philosophical statement that was germane to his professional training. It was the word "cultivate" that helped pull together the other four components of my system on *psycho-cultivation*. I now believe, when people fulfill their purpose to serve and to provide their skills, talents and experiences, they at some level understand the five secrets of *psycho-cultivation*.

Personally, I understood the word "cultivate" in a more tangible way that led me to seek answers from an unbiased source. This unbiased source which stems from memories of granddaddy's cultivating the land was vivid in my mind. These memories, are pleasantly, with me at all times, but their connection with this concept was submerged until now. It made all the things I have been studying relevant to me! The answer was right there on the farm, a source from my environment. The connection was in understanding the transformation vegetation goes through when the land is cultivated and seeds planted. The plant's life, from the moment it rests in the ground to its production later in its life, led me to this new concept. This understanding excited me and helped me to focus on the ideas that led me to a concept I call psycho-cultivation.

Psycho-cultivation: Its Meaning

People want to achieve the fulfillment of their dreams and to have a sense of purpose in their lives. It may be to break a cycle of negative experiences. Or, it may be to achieve a dream home or a better life-style. However, few are willing to accept the fact that in order to do so, personal change is required. The change, also, requires one to have a purpose, to realize a vision, and to have dreams and goals to fulfill that purpose. *Psycho-cultivation* has reference to spiritual principles involving serving and providing skills and talents which are used to acquire a productive state of mind.

Psycho-cultivation is becoming your best through the process of uprooting, changing and replacing negative thought pictures by psychologically nurturing and acting on the following attitudes: to have a purpose to serve others and to provide skills and talents, to act on a vision, to improve oneself through personal growth, to overcome adversity and to become productive in life. These can only be achieved with the power of faith. With faith, people will believe in the existence of new desired positive thought pictures which will enable them to fulfill their purpose to serve. Also, *psycho-cultivation* helps them to live in harmony with others through contributing and achieving personal dreams and goals.

In short, *psycho-cultivation* changes the way people think. It allows them to keenly concentrate on what they want or the object of their desire. When I was a youngster, I would say or do nothing in public that would draw attention to me or my ideas. Even though I had some good ideas, I was shy and did not think highly of myself. I had low self-esteem, as well as low self-image. I have noticed how *psycho-cultivation* works in my life which caused me to change.

Improving My Self-image

As a youth, I did not have much confidence in myself. I desired to change. During my quest for personal change, a new revelation unfolded. I discovered my predicament was not any more unique than anyone else's. I realized that other people felt just as I did. Given the fact that my situation was not unique, I decided to change more than ever.

Later in life, I believed I could change my self-image. I started reading religious books and self-help material. I traveled, earned higher educational degrees, and talked to successful people in order to gain from them an attitude about success. I experienced adversity and worked through them. I learned to be proud of my heritage. I started to believe in myself and to know that I, as well as my ideas, mattered. Because of my faith, I began to believe these new revelations about myself. I started focusing on this new positive self-image. I started claiming and believing that these new qualities were already in existence and a part of my present self-image.

My psychological transformation did not happen instantly. It took place over a period of years, but one day I realized that, through seeds of faith which I planted years before, I had become that person. In my quest to live a productive life, to find my purpose to serve and to fulfill that purpose, I discovered my pattern for success. It took all five attitudes for success in my formula, activating and working in concert, for me to begin to live a life of purpose according to my system of *psycho-cultiva-*

tion. The full concept did not reveal itself to me until I realized and understood the final two principles—adversity and productivity. When people learn early in life the five attitudes for success of *psycho-cultivation* their poor self-image and self-esteem will begin to vanish.

Insurance Against Adversity

The principle of *psycho-cultivation* begins with having a purpose to serve, to provide talents and to create the proper thought pictures to fulfill that purpose. Your desires in life, which are accomplished through the fruits of your labor, should be aligned with your purpose to serve. A continuity check must be done for every new and old vision to determine whether your efforts are aligned with your purpose. Training must be done for self-improvement so that when adversities are encountered, they are acknowledged as you move on to produce the kind of results your purpose requires.

The concept of *psycho-cultivation* works well with adversity. It involves realizing that you need to change to overcome adversity and to continue toward achievement. It is a concept built on acknowledging and considering adversities and not the avoidance of them. If adversities occur, you should acknowledge their existence and use them for your benefit.

Psycho-cultivation gets you mentally tough so you can subdue your problems. When you use the powerful attitudes for success, it reinforces the idea of having a purpose to serve and of fulfilling that purpose. The farmer's purpose is revealed when he or she produces goods or provides a service. A doctor serves by providing medical care service. Although these services differ, they are all ways to serve.

On the farm, cow manure is often used as compost—another name for fertilizer—to enrich the soil. Fertilizer is like a catalyst for vegetative growth. Therefore, consider using adversity as a fertilizer and as a catalyst of growth and success for people. People need to adopt the attitude that personal adversities should inspire them to change for the better. Whether change occurs for positive growth, for a setback or for a change back to normalcy, the situation should cause them to reflect, discover lessons learned and consider changing. If someone comes from a dysfunctional family, has been abused, or has abused drugs, the person must realize these are past experiences which cannot be changed. The goal of *psycho-cultivation* is to get that person to begin to view these experiences now as fertilizer for future growth and success.

After I was exonerated from the "Texas Nightmare," I had to decide what to do with this "compost" of an experience. The pain, suffering and experiences surrounding my wrongful incarceration in the Texas penal system were immense. I decided to use my emotional pain and depravation as "fertilizer" by sharing my concern, by desiring to educate and inform others in order to help them overcome and achieve their dreams.

Psycho-cultivation can work, but it takes changing and accepting that you have God-given qualities which are to serve humanity. It is realizing that God will not allow anything to happen to His people that they cannot bear. When adversities occur, they should be treated as a reminder to focus on your dream and to move forward toward your vision. Adversities are a small part of a larger and more meaningful and satisfying vision for you. Adversities, viewed properly, are like weights to a weight lifter, or rocks to a mountain climber—they are a part of your success process.

Circumstances in people's lives may be good or bad. Therefore, they should make a concerted effort to always focus on positive outcomes to bring closure to circumstances which impact negatively in life—represents change. This change simply cancels out the negative circumstance. It allows people to mature and to grow spiritually, intellectually, and emotionally as a result of these changes. It allows people to cultivate personal dreams. These dreams can serve as motivation to accomplish that which is important to them. Also, these dreams will motivate them to improve their lives by studying and by listening to experts who have achieved in their prospective area of concentration.

People need insurance against adversities. This can be accomplished by maintaining a positive attitude and employing *Psycho-cultivation* when confronted with negative circumstances. Finally, they must fulfill the purpose and dreams that are in their hearts regardless of the price as long as they do not hurt or destroy other people.

Thought Pictures

Thought pictures are mental images that are visualized in one's mind. They can be images of goals or dreams. Also, they can be images of fear or of impending disaster. Thought pictures have been the most powerful force behind the dreams of great people. Your thoughts, can mainly, come from yourself or other people's thoughts motivated by their plans, dreams and goals. Your thoughts are like seeds that are buried in the rich soil of your memories. When you think of a desired dream often, you will want it to become real. If you have a big dream for which you are willing to work and sacrifice, your rewards will be big.

Your thoughts are what control your destiny. What you focus on enlarges and attracts similar circumstances in your lives. People think in pictures. These pictures are thought pictures. Thoughts in the form of pictures are stored in your memory, which contribute toward your belief, attitude and behavioral toward life.

Think about a red apple. What did you visualize? Of course, the red apple was visualized. This is an illustration of a thought picture. Obviously, the words were not seen. However, the pictures that you see mentally, such as a door, book, and fire are all thought pictures produced from your mind. There are many circumstances in life both good and bad which may bring a man or woman to a crossroad wherein they decide what their perspective will be. If they choose to view the circumstance as negative, their perspective and outlook may be negative. Conversely, if they choose to view every situation as having a positive side to it, their outlook will be positive and they will operate from a position of strength. The main factor which tilts people's attitude or perspective from positive to negative is their dominant thought pictures.

I was thinking one Sunday evening about thought pictures. I wondered how I could conceptualize thought pictures so that people could visualize them. I thought for a moment, "What if one's thoughts are charged either negatively or positively? Assume that the "I can do it" thoughts are charged positively and the "I can't do it" thoughts are charged negatively. What if it were possible for these charged thoughts pictures to be collected and placed in separate baskets? Next, they would be separated depending on whether or not a thought is positive (self enhancing) or negative (destructive)? Now, assume that the more numerous basket of the two decides a person's behavior, outlook on life and eventually his or her destiny? Believe it or not, your perspective and outlook on life comes about from the way you process and label your circumstances as either positive or negative. The label that appears the most will shape your attitude, perspective, and outlook on life.

If in your imagination most of the thought pictures in the basket are negative, you will be doubtful in decision-making and gloomy in your outlook on life. You will think that you can't make ends meet. You will think that you will not get the job. You will believe that other people are more intelligent. You may feel that you are being held back because of your color. Perhaps you will believe that there's but so much opportunity. You're too old. You don't have an education, so there is no use trying or attempting to earn a degree. It is easy to imagine how this person, with such "hang-ups," might choose to make negative decisions.

If, on the other hand, most of the thought pictures in the basket are positive, you will use faith in your decision-making and be optimistic in your outlook on life. Therefore, your faith will give you the comfort to believe that you can have self-efficacy. You will believe that you will get the job you are pursuing because you are as capable or as intelligent as the next person. You will believe that your desires, skills, knowledge and attitude move you forward and the color of your skin can never impede your progress. You will believe that opportunity is everywhere! You will believe that the mental capacity to desire new possibilities never ages; therefore, you are never too old in thought. You will earn an education and you will believe that you have every reason to try, because trying gives you a chance to win!

A Source of Positive Identity

Knowing yourself and allowing positive thought pictures of yourself are a major step toward understanding what you are capable of becoming. I perform workshops in school systems and I often come across some interesting revelations. When I talk with students, I soon observe in some cases the following: a lack of maturity, a need for home training, the lack of a positive self concept, a negative attitude toward authority, a problematic attitude and the need to have positive educational goals and dreams.

The students need positive thought pictures as a source of good identity. Having a positive identity is important to their opinion of themselves or to what they are capable of achieving. If they believe that they came from a less than desirable heritage, it does not matter, because they can get the facts. They cannot allow themselves to succumb to a belief generated by someone with ulterior motives who feels that their heritage is inferior or undesirable. If they choose to believe that they are inferior, they need to take this up with God.

All of God's creatures are always first class! No one should choose to believe that he or she is a second class person. Get rid of this thinking because it suggests God made a mistake with you, your color and your heritage. Unless you accept inferiority, no one can force an inferiority complex upon you; unless, you are a willing vessel. Unless you become a willing vessel, their slurs, taunts and criticisms will not have an affect on you.

Don't accept the negative input from negative people who spread negative messages about what you are capable of doing. Instead, think of yourself as person who has the awesome potential to serve, who is unique and who is productive. What is most important is to learn to use your personal hereditary and background to your advantage. If you have people in your family who are wasting themselves away on alcohol and drugs, it doesn't have to be your future. Refuse to abuse drugs! You posses the power to refuse to allow alcohol or drugs to control your life.

If people's ancestors were presidents of the United States, slaves or immigrants, theirs lineages had a spark of greatness at one time or another if you are willing to search carefully. Most people ancestry tried to make sure that your future would be better than theirs. They were strong, brave, and intelligent people whose goals were to be survivors. As immigrants, they arrived in this country willingly as free persons or unwillingly as slaves, with big dreams or hopes of freedom and prosperity for their families.

Affecting Behavior through Thought Pictures

Over one million people are incarcerated in the prisons and jails of America. This staggering number of inmates have separated themselves from society through their criminal activities. They allowed an "attitude of a taker" to be their dominant thought pictures which, in turn, affected their behavior. The solution begins with educating parents to recognize that their children are perhaps mirroring their behavior, their peers behavior or the behavior of people on the streets and on television. The things that children do are not ideas created in a vacuum. Therefore, virtues must be made part of the family life-style and must be respected by family members. You should always practice a positive life-style, maintain high principles and be virtuous in order to serve as good *community examples* (role models).

Parents must properly address young people's exposure to those elements in society that may impact them negatively. They should monitor the input coming from friends, television, and radio and especially those advertisements which suggest societal vices such as illegal drugs, violence and etc. These views will adversely reflect, if allowed, their family's value. If negative thought pictures from these media are left alone to grow in the minds of our youths, like seeds in the ground, they will grow and produce. We have to work on our loved ones thinking—their thought pictures. Change these thought pictures, and the behavior will change.

If youths are made to believe that they are inferior to others, then they will rebel in order to justify their actions. They may not respect society's code of ethics or adhere to its way of achieving success. Society has a code of conduct which is its way of doing things. For example, there is a dress code at the office. Similarly, English is the communication code for professionals in the market place of America.

There are many codes involving how you do things, how you respect other people's property, etc. because society wants you to respect its venues. We need to accept people outside our societal system and bring them in and work with them. If you make disenfranchised people welcome, they may change. If they become part of our institution, they will not likely attack something they are a part of.

Youngsters should be made to realize that they are responsible for their actions. Our youth need to be educated and trained with the attitudes and beliefs needed to become self-supportive and productive citizens. Because they are being fed input from all sources that they are mischievous, ugly, unqualified and lazy, they will internalize these thought pictures. This negative input, which is from their environment, is unconventional, and can only lead to unconventional behavior. If they succumb to the input, their behavior becomes unconventional and they may choose a pathway which separates them from society. They may turn on society and live a life as a people who take from others. We want them to believe that there are conventional and legal options for them to execute and achieve their dreams.

Youths who believe that their earned qualifications will not permit them to make a living in society because of their race, creed, color, sexual orientation, or gender, will not take full advantage of their options nor will they reach their full potential. They will believe that real success in huge proportions are reserved for certain people or those who are wealthy. People refuse to view life that permit "road blocks" or biases, also don't believe that their options are unlimited and their dreams attainable.

The way to change negative thought pictures in our youth is to start within the family. In the family, children must be told that their purpose is to serve and to provide skills and talents. They should be told that there will be adversities hindering the fulfillment of their dreams. However, they can prevail! Adversities don't represent stop signs. Instead, they represent "move forward with caution" indicators which should move us forward. The key is exposure. The family must expose children to a variety of experiences that encourage growth and a positive self identity. *Psycho-cultivation* is a powerful model which can mold an individual into having a positive self-identity—replete with structure and direction. When you are sold on the idea that you can control your life, use the five attitudes for success for guidance.

PART 2

Attitude For Success #1:

Acquiring a Purpose

Purpose

One's purposes on this earth are to serve others, to contribute talents and skills, to benefit people, and to fulfill our goals. A tomato seed's first stage, the purpose stage, starts when it is placed in the ground, which is the launching of the seed's destiny. Before the seed was placed into the ground, it had only potential. The seed's potential is manifested through its life's purpose which is to produce.

The seed, at the moment of creation, had the genetic coding capability to fulfill its purpose—to produce a tomato. It is as if the seed had been pre-programmed to understand what it has to go through to achieve its purpose. When the seed was in the container among other seeds, it did not grow. When it was on the shelf, it did not grow. The seed grew when it was taken out of the container; when it was removed from the shelf and placed into the ground. It seems as if God, the Spiritual Intelligence, programmed the seed to become activated under these definite conditions.

The seed needs to be placed in its environment among the soil, water, nutrients and adversities in order to pursue its destiny. It has a pre-programmed purpose from the start and a destiny to fulfill. The purpose of the plant is manifested by the fruit it produces, a product that serves people, as well as a way to reproduce.

Humans have the inherent ability to use their thought seeds (thoughts) to program themselves so as to make their own decisions. They decide whether to possess the attitude of a server or the attitude of a taker. The seed's life purpose is to serve, by producing a product that it does not consume or from which it does not directly benefit. Humans come along, as well as animals and insects and consume the product that the plant bears.

CHAPTER 4

Serving Others and Providing Skills and Talents

Our purpose

All people have a purpose in life which is to serve one another. Whatever occupation they decide to undertake to fulfill their purpose is their prerogative. If they do not serve a useful purpose, they are resigned to serve a purpose out of step with the universe. The minister, dog catcher, and farmer all serve purposes in the community. The minister's purpose is to serve by providing spiritual services. The dog catcher's purpose is to serve by catching stray dogs and other animals. The farmer serves by producing food. Everyone ends up serving a purpose, a purpose by design or by default.

The Principle of Serving

The principle of serving states that human beings must have a purpose to serve themselves and others by providing their skills and talents in order to become productive in society. An ant's mound is a good example of cooperative working and serving. All ants in the colony are cooperating because in each ant there is an instinctive purpose to serve, which is the propagation of the species. Some ants provide food, or some guard the colony and others the unborn. The next generation is the beneficiary of those services.

If people are serving time in prison for stealing, they are there for violating the law of serving. Their negative and selfish motives were designed to benefit and serve no other than themselves. When they stole, their stealing did not serve the general welfare of other people.

Understanding the Purpose to Serve

Purpose is the intention or reason for the existence of something. One's purpose for doing something always reveals one's deeds or actions. Purpose can also justify motives or actions. Purpose makes known why things are the way they are. It is the source for experiencing pleasure or pain. When you finally realize the purpose behind a behavior, and how it controls you, you understand why you behave the way you do. Your expertise and the things you do well, naturally, as well as unknown skills and talents, may reveal what your true purpose to serve should be.

Humans are good at inventing and designing things. The tall skyscrapers, huge earth-moving machinery and fast airplanes were invented and designed by humans. Yet, the skyscrapers don't touch the sky and earth-moving machinery can't move the earth. The Spiritual Intelligence, God, can do all of these things because He created everything that we see and can't see. God is the reason everything exists. It was all done by Him. All that the Spiritual Intelligence created was created to serve His purposes. Whether you serve His will or your will, you are still *serving*, but to what end? Also humans, unlike God, invent and design objects because humans desire to have their intellectual modifications of God's creation to serve themselves. There is nothing wrong with improving and making life comfortable. Our ultimate goal should be to make these inventions and designs serve God and other people.

Have you wondered how difficult it would be to create a human body, animals, the sun, or even the billions of galaxies? You can speculate on what the purpose of most of these entities is. However, God knows their purposes, and their purposes may be beyond our ability to comprehend. The sunlight benefits plants, animals, and people. The sun holds the earth in its gravitational pull. If the sun did not hold us in its gravitational pull, the earth would be slung into the coldness of outer space. Everything that exists from moment to moment is part of some grand purpose which is to serve.

Committing to a Purpose to Serve

Having a life's purpose and being committed to that purpose helps to keep you on course. A purpose helps you to prioritize and act on things needing to be done in your life. While working to achieve a goal, life will test your resolve. As long as you make plans for the outcome to be positive, then "nine times out of ten" nothing can stop you from realizing a positive result.

Looking back on my childhood, I understand now how important a commitment to purpose was for my parents. They had to be committed to rearing eight children. We lived on about one acre and a half of land in the beautiful countryside of Denmark, South Carolina, in an old wooden house with reddish, imitation brick siding. We had a large household which consisted of four generations. My great-grandmother, grandmother, grandfather, mother, stepfather, four sisters, three brothers, two cousins and I comprised the members of our household.

The house was surrounded by light brown, beach-like soil in which no grass grew. In the large gardens which were on both sides of the house, we planted long rows of corn, string beans, peas, okra, and tomatoes. My younger brothers, James Willis, Jr. and Ricky Willis, and cousin Joseph Islar enjoyed eating the fresh fruits and vegetables from the garden. In the rear of our house was a well that quenched our thirst after walking, running and exploring the thick, green forest behind our house. Before the evening was over, we had to feed the pigs, cut wood and replenish the well water which was stored in the house and used for cooking, drinking, bathing and washing clothes.

From this meager, yet nurturing and challenging upbringing, I observed life's adversities first hand. Adversities challenged the grown-ups' commitment to purpose on the farm. I noticed many adversities granddaddy had to withstand when nature tested his garden with harsh weather. His purpose on the farm evolved around providing for his family. Regardless of the circumstances, he committed himself to achieving this purpose.

I learned commitment to purpose and to positive thinking from learning the value of work through participation. Granddaddy planted the crops with faith and a positive attitude that they would grow and produce. He demonstrated his faith by planting crops, digging-up weeds, and doing whatever was necessary for them to have a chance to survive. Acting on faith implies commitment. Having faith was an integral part of granddaddy's achieving his purpose since it involved taking action toward a purpose. The work that he generated was the result of his belief. granddaddy's commitment to his purpose was manifested by the flourishing of his garden each year.

Finding Your Purpose to Serve

In finding your purpose, you have to believe that your core purpose is to serve people. Even people who love some people and hate others seem willing to serve the ones they love. These same people who are declared enemies will at times, when the relationship is mended or in an emergency, help an enemy. I am reminded of the Cold War that existed between the United States and Russia and how each of these countries maintained a relationship which was at best reserved with each other. When the forty years of the Cold War ended between the countries, a new willingness to serve in a relationship of progress occurred through joint space ventures, economic support and business ventures.

The manner in which you choose to serve others is left to you. An employee of Burger King Restaurant serves the public by selling hamburgers. The owner of the supermarket serves his or her purpose by selling food to the customers. Each of these businesses was started by an enterprising person wanting to provide these types of services to the public.

In your quest to find your purpose to serve, you must examine yourself and put down on paper all of your assets. You must include all of the things that you like doing and even what you don't like doing. Include the tribulations that you have gone through and the blessings or miracles that you have received as a result. A tribulation can often be turned around into an asset or a blessing for other people. Choose from this list of all of your experiences, skills, interests and dreams to determine the best way you can serve others that will bring satisfaction to you. Though your purpose to serve may be inconvenient, troublesome or difficult, if you keep moving forward, in the end you will achieve your dreams. Your success will be worth the effort and the purpose you are seeking will become known to you.

Controlling Success or Failure

I mentioned earlier, if your positive and negative thought pictures could be placed in separate baskets, the basket with the most positive or negative thought pictures would determine your attitude. If the positive thoughts become the majority, your attitude will be positive. With this in mind, it is vital that you maintain a positive attitude because people respond better to those with a positive attitude. If you are in business and you serve everyone with a pleasing and wanting-to-serve attitude, your business will flourish. People follow those people or work for businesses which are willing to go the extra mile in providing quality service.

An attitude of quality service will decide, to a greater extent, your success. A positive or negative attitude, automatically, pulls you in its direction, because what you think about most of the time becomes your conditioning which essentially determines your direction or path in life.

Whenever you try to change your path in life, your dominant thought pictures, and your conditioning, really make the decision for you. It's similar to being on autopilot. One of the main reasons people stop trying is that their conditioning casts a shadow of doubt. If your business is not doing well, you first need to change. You need to change your attitude about how you service people. Among all of the things that can cause a business to do poorly, poor service is the most frequent culprit when employees are not willing to go the extra mile in providing quality service.

If you have allowed an attitude of poverty to be your main focus, because that is all you have seen in your environment, you will continue to exist in your current circumstances. You can change! An attitude of poverty will not improve your service which will not improve your circumstances. This attitude will tend to cause you to cut back on your services, which will affect your business and profit line adversely.

It takes having an attitude of prosperity for you to work yourself out of undesirable circumstances. Get to the point where you believe if you can imagine the thought picture in your mind, it is possible to possess it in reality. Don't be bothered about what others say about your dreams and your potential. If it is legal and it does not hurt anyone, go for it! You only fail if you don't put in an honest effort. When you improve your services, the quality of your service will invariably cause your income to rise and your dreams to become a reality. Remember you only fail when you fail to try!

PART 3

Attitude for Success #2:

Activating Vision with Desire and Motivation

Vision

The tomato seed's second stage, the vision stage, started at the point when it was created. The internal picture of what the tomato is to become was within its genetic makeup at its inception. The vision of the tomato seed, putting it in human terms, is to produce tomatoes for anyone's use. The vision was not of the tomato's choosing; it was God's, the Spiritual Intelligence of the universe.

Imagine the dreams of the tomato seed. Picture it saying, "I can't wait to be placed into the ground. I heard that when you are buried in the ground, you'll be in tomato heaven. The adventure makes it worthwhile. There is the subduing of the adversities *and the many challenges leading up to the dream of becoming a big, red, juicy tomato!"*

A tomato plant has to be durable because of the experiences leading up to the fulfillment of its destiny. The proper attitude for success was coded in its genes. The seedling somehow knows its destiny. All of its life, it has been maturing and growing for the following process: to be buried in the ground and to experience loneliness and isolation. Using a considerable amount of effort in displacing the soil, the seedling is now prepared to break through the surface of the ground. Once this feat is accomplished, there are overwhelming assaults from birds, rain, weeds, drought, wind and humans. Finally, the tomato experiences the exhilaration of fulfilling its purpose. Each time you *see a tomato on the vine, the vision encoded in its genes by the Creator has been manifested.*

A person, however, must have a vision. A person's vision must be designed to fulfill personal needs yet broad enough to serve others. It is not useful to others to have a vision which does not include bringing someone else along. Every time people become involved in a winner's vision, their effort also builds on their vision and *also contributes toward the winner's vision. Maybe one day, these people will expand their personal visions and cause them to grow into a grand enterprise.*

CHAPTER 5

Activating Your Vision, Dreams and Goals

Perceive and Believe in Dreams

You must begin to view adversities in the landscape of your vision as experiences or adventures that motivate. The accomplishment of the dreams within your vision will be difficult, but you will begin to acquire all of them. When you are on a roller coaster going down twisting, turning out of control, this is no fun. Having no dream, is the way some people have chosen, by default, to live their lives—twisting, turning out of control.

However, when living your life with a vision, your roller coaster experience may still have its ups and downs, but you know what the outcome should be. You can ride the roller coaster adventure of life because you know where you get on, the scope of the ride, and where you get off. When you live your life from a dream plan, you can anticipate a fair degree of adversities, yet the dream beckons you on.

You have to conceive the desires of your heart with the faith that they will become a reality in your life. We have heard the saying, "If you can conceive it, you can achieve it." This saying is very applicable. Though, there is a deeper meaning to the word achieve. In order to achieve the dreams conceived in your mind, they have to be reinforced with a strong self-image. Most people have a strong dream. It's the self-image that prevents them from realizing the fruits of their dreams. One of the best ways to build up the self-image is to say affirmations. Such affirmations are these: "I have confidence in myself;" "I believe in myself;" or "I can do it!" Once the self-image is all built-up and healthy, then you can begin to believe.

Believing is the signal to your subconscious mind that you possess the confidence to follow through. You will not move forward unless you believe that you can do it. Your self-image has to be strong and you must believe in yourself. If you believe that what you have conceived can become a reality, you can acquire it. So off you go on the journey toward your dreams. As soon as you get going, you will run into fear or problems. Fear is the opposite of faith. It has no business being in your pathway. It is there because it wants to test your companion which is faith. Fear will leave as soon as you convince your subconscious mind that your faith is strong and real to you.

After fear has left, you will often run into adversities. Adversities are also a test of your resolve. They are there to make us think there is no use trying because all seems to be lost. You have to look for the equivalent blessing. Once you go for it, you will notice that adversities will submit and become your stepping stone.

Once you have conceived an idea and your belief has been tested, the final stage is the reward. Once the reward is in view it is a lot easier to acquire because it does not take faith anymore, you can see it. It is visible and within your reach. All that is needed is to possess it! If anything challenges your right to possess the dream, you should be mindful that you conceive it, believe it, and you can achieve it! This illustration highlights the whole process I have been discussing. Like the tomato seed, we must be willing to work through adversities and achieve our purposes. It is training your thoughts to create a powerful vision to serve and to fuel your goals and dreams. Learn to create dreams and goals by writing out a plan of action and a blueprint to forge your vision.

In Attitude for Success Number Two, activate your vision of success with desire and motivation, the already cultivated mental grounds of the mind are used to build dreams and goals. Coexisting with your vision are adversities which are like unwanted weeds in a garden. *Psycho-cultivation* rids one of negative and unproductive thoughts like the unwanted weeds in a garden.

In engineering, I used to conceive an object mentally for a client and put it on paper for the technician to use as a blueprint to build. I transformed the client's idea into thought pictures. I made the thought pictures real by designing them on the computer or on the drawing board. My design was reproduced on the blueprint machine. If the client was satisfied with the drawings, everyone signed off and the technician began constructing the client's dream.

For your vision to become real, you must be able to live your dreams mentally, to walk in your dream home; to drive your beautiful car, to sail in your yacht, and to take the drive to the airport to begin your eagerly anticipated vacation. The work and effort it takes for your dreams to become a reality may involve making contact with your customer base, getting into the environment of your dreams, or revisiting your dreams. A tomato seed has a pre-programmed genetic coded blueprint of its final configuration. It wasn't until the tomato seed was in the ground, in the thick of it all and in contact with the environment, that it became activated. Therefore, you have to follow your dream plans, to get into your distinct environment and to work it until your dreams becomes a reality.

Dream Desires

A vision consists of images of dreams (things) that you want to realize. The vision includes all of the little dreams and goals you desire. The vision is the big picture. The vision includes the totality of the piece parts—the dreams plus the goals. These individual dreams and goals become motivators for you to achieve the state of prosperity which your vision requires. When you envision yourself in a state of prosperity, this vision suggests that you believe you are worthy of the best life has to offer. However, if you decide not to envision a life of prosperity and growth for you or your family, then you will become a worker at the mercy of someone else's vision.

Included within the framework of one's vision may be a beautiful home, a sizable bank account, a happy family, an airplane, a vacation and volunteer work. The vision, once acted upon, will activate your desire for your dreams and cause them to happen.

It is best to pursue these dreams one at a time. Once you decide to chase a dream, make sure it will enrich the lives of people. The capability of the dream to enrich the lives of many people is what causes you to become rich. When working for a company in a cooperative setting, your ability to help lots of people is shared with others; consequently, you seldom become wealthy. The owner of the company, the risk-taker or dreamer, rightfully earns the wealth. The dream has to be yours; you have to become the dreamer and render a benefit or service to a multitude of people before you become wealthy.

A goal is specific while a dream is not specific. The goal is like a stop along the way, because it refreshes and it motivates you to continue toward our dreams. The vision is that state of being hoped for—the image that includes all of their dreams. The size of your dreams will determine the degree of your prosperity. Your prosperity will always start within your imagination long before your success becomes a reality. For some, prosperity might be at the income level of $30,000 and to another it might start at $2,000,000.

Dream desires help to release your potential because they help to bring out your inner abilities. They inspire you to have something, to be more, and to do more. Dreams are an inborn source of power and potential that help you to become your best. Success starts with having a desire for something you don't possess and pursuing it until it becomes yours.

Dream Motivation

A dream motivation is an important and benevolent desire in your life. An important dream motivation will remain an obsession until you possess it. The dream motivation occupies every moment of your productive and unproductive thinking. It's the dominant desire that you know that you will possess.

My strongest dream motivation occurred when my freedom was lost for sixteen months. I was sentenced to life in prison due to a mistaken arrest and conviction. Everyone to whom I was closely connected plus my freedom and career were forcibly taken from me. My dream motivation was to clear my name and gain my freedom.

My dream motivation was clear. I imagined myself as a free man again. I visualized tasting seafood and driving my Volkswagen again. I imagined smelling roses and the aroma of other spring plants. I envisioned the green spring countryside as a free man. I desired freedom more intensely each day.

My dreams were transformed into goals when my attorneys and I made specific, measurable, realistic, written and meaningful plans in the form of legal briefs. These goals were tied to court dates for me to address my wrongful imprisonment. I relied on faith and belief in God to keep me going. I focused on what I was going to do when I was freed. I learned to rebuke negative thoughts through my belief in God, the words of the scriptures and the blessings which I believed would come to me. Lastly, I was determined that I would never quit until I was vindicated and because of my faith and tenacity, I was.

The mind should always be focused on a positive dream. Without a positive dream to direct us, we move by default in a direction away from our purpose. A dream motivation gives you power to help you achieve your purpose. A dream lets you know that you are headed in the right direction.

Everything that was built by people was a product of their dreams. You can dream large or small dreams and if you believe you can achieve them, you can bring them into existence. The mind has millions of brain cells that are being used to serve human beings in carrying out their desires. Make sure that most of those brain cells receive positive input. It's time to take advantage of these brain cells by getting them to work for you. You must think positively by believing that your dream can become a manifested part of your life.

From Claiming and Believing Dreams to Realizing Goals

In the early nineteenth century when the West was being settled, the settlers would stake out a claim on a piece of property. They would stake off the property and file for ownership of the plot of land. After they received the ownership paperwork, the land became theirs to do with as they pleased.

Claiming or believing a goal is the tool that cultivates the mental grounds to bring about change, a change which encourages a more productive, giving and serving attitude. Claiming and believing in the spiritual sense represents staking out mental dreams, and knowing that even before they are manifested, whether there are good times or bad times, the dreams will be achieved.

Spiritually, dreams enable you to use the power of faith to take ownership of dreams or goals. It is stepping out on faith and believing that the dreams of your heart will become yours one day. People who are successful in claiming and believing their goals usually believe that God supports their claim to their dreams.

Claiming and believing is powerful because dreams are spiritually bundled together with faith, belief, action and positive thought pictures of yourself already possessing your desires. It is knowing that you have it, and it is knowing that you deserve it because God is willing to give good things to His children. You know that He will answer you because your heart's desire is to serve.

Thought pictures of prosperity may be a life-style of financial independence, education for your children, travel, or helping others. It is claiming and believing ownership of the dream, the thought pictures of what you want that help to motivate you when it seems that it is not worth the effort.

Three Steps to Setting Powerful Goals

A goal is nothing unless it means something to you. It has to become an ever present thought—a dominant thought—in your mind. Your goals have to be carried out in a well thought out and orderly plan. You are about to learn my three-step system to setting powerful and meaningful goals for your future. The three steps are important because they are part of a process for all realized dreams. They are as follows: Thinking of Dreams Desired, Paying The Price For Your Dreams and Continuing The Journey With New Dreams and Goals.

Step One:
Think of Dreams Desired

Convert Dreams to Goals

Dreams are desires to accomplish something you value. Once they are accomplished, you continue to seek new dreams and goals. Accomplishing dreams requires belief, setting goals and paying the price; however, an important ingredient in manifesting dreams requires believing that you are worthy to acquire them. Dreams don't happen instantly; they take time. Therefore, you must have lots of dreams that you want to be realized because some will come true sooner than others. With every dream there will be a price you have to pay.

I had a dream, a dream of becoming an engineer, but it was in jeopardy because of fear. When I was in college, I used to dread going to Daisy Dunn Johnson's Career Development class. I liked the instructor, but I didn't like speaking in front of people. My goal was to learn to speak in front of my fellow students. Knowing that Mrs. Johnson could call on me at any time, I had to know the subject matter. When she did call on me, I would stumble through the speech in a state of fear. The driving force that propelled me to complete the goal and to realize my dream was being a senior and needing the credits to graduate. I had to complete this course to graduate which also caused me to accomplish my dream. Years later, I gained the confidence and enrolled in a Toastmaster's club which improved my presentation skills.

Set Strategies for Goals

A dream becomes a goal by first writing it down on paper and making the dream specific. There is something powerful about putting your goals on paper. In America, some of our most precious documents, The Declaration of Independence and the Constitution of the United States of America, were written on paper by the founding fathers of this nation. These documents are very important and profound to millions of Americans.

The founding fathers specified what freedoms they wanted for Americans by writing their demands down in that famous document we call The Declaration of Independence. They made it measurable at the moment of the signing of The Declaration of Independence, the time frame for independence was at once. Realistic demands, such as, "No taxation without representation," among others, fueled their cry for independence. The desire for independence was meaningful to millions within the Colonies. Because their quest was meaningful to them, they placed their lives, liberty and the pursuit of happiness on the line. In the end, the British challenged their resolve and the Colonies won.

If a goal is worth writing down, the specifics have to be known; you need to know what you are pursuing. Once you know exactly what you want, there has to be a way to measure your progress. The goal has to be realistic as to the time-frame or whether it can be humanly done. It has to be emotionally tied to you. It has to mean something to you. Then the dream is transformed into a goal by making it specific, measurable, realistic, and meaningful. A strategy for making a goal specific is to picture the goal mentally as it would be on the day it is to be accomplished. On that day, envision making this statement, "I made the commitment to accomplish this goal on this month, day and year." When making your goal measurable, think in terms of how much, to what extent or what duration. To make your goals realistic, think about whether it is humanly possible to meet the demands of time, money, and dependency. Then consider whether or not it is worth putting forth the effort. When a goal is meaningful to you, the emotions and feelings are involved in all of your projects. Strong emotions mean the goal really means something to you.

CHARACTER BENCHMARK LESSON # 2:
Developing a Goal Plan of Action

An important first step in realizing your dreams involves developing a plan. For example, a plan to become self-employed, should justify why you're giving up time, money, and effort in pursuit of greater flexibility is necessary. The possibility of wealth or a secure life style is usually adequate motivation for most people to follow a well thought out plan of action.

You need to separate major goals in your life by prioritizing them. The model below will help you develop a plan so as to clarify your goals in all areas of your life. The following directions and the examples will assist you in writing the four components of a goal plan of action (dreams, goals, affirmations and a goal plan of action) into one format, a *goal plan* for all eight areas of your life.

Directions:

a. List as many as 35 dreams in the Appendix A of the book that you want to posses or experience in your lifetime. Select one dream from this list for each of the eight categories of life and write them down in the appropriate sections before.
b. Transform the dream into a goal by making the dream specific, measurable, realistic, and meaningful to you.
c. Rewrite the goal into a positive statement, an affirmation as shown in the example below.
d. Write a plan of action using the simple three-steps plan leading up to its accomplishment.
e. Complete a decision statement.

Example:

a. Degree in science (*Write one important educational dream you want to accomplish.)*
b. Educational goal: I will earn a science degree by January 1, 2010. (Transform your dream into a goal by making the dream specific; including the month, day, and year in the statement).
c. Educational affirmation: I am excited about earning a science degree. (Rewrite the goal into an affirmation—an advance goal declaration).
d. Plan of action: Write a simple three-steps plan of action to accomplish your goal:
   Step 1. Enroll in college
   Step 2. Earn a 3.5 grade point average
   Step 3. Graduate from college
e. Decision statement: To accomplish this goal (educational), I am committing 3 days (how many days) a week toward making it a reality. My reward (something that you want) for accomplishing this goal is a trip to New York. After completing this goal, my next educational goal is: to earn a Master's Degree in Biology.

1. **Educational Goal.** Education is one of the most valuable tools in helping to fulfill your dreams. There are many institutions of higher learning from which to receive a quality education. The traditional ways are to enroll in a college, a university, or a technical college. Some of the less formal ways of acquiring an education or additional training is to get on-the-job-training, or to exchange information with others through networking. Learning is an ongoing process. Whenever you are learning, you are being taught by a teacher. Everybody has a message; therefore, you should listen discriminatingly for the purpose of learning. Listening is especially important for the family. Family members are like computer operators. They are responsible for the data entries (values) that influences the lives of their children.

Before the technological era, it was easier for people without a formal education to become wealthy. For these people to become successful today, they will have to be technologically astute or hire someone who is competent. Today, the computer can fax data in minutes or secure an airline ticket. All of this can be done from the comfort of your home. Using the computer, information can be retrieved from universities, organizations or businesses from around the world. You can keep up with your finances more easily and checkup on your stocks or even place an order. To be successful, one should be abreast of current technology. If you don't take advantage of the market place, your competition will take advantage of it. Education is part of the growth process which involves changing and improving intellectually in order to be competitive in the market place.

a. Educational dreams: ______________________________
   (Write one important educational dream)
b. Educational *goal:* I will earn a/an __________________
   degree by (when) __________________________________
c. Educational *affirmation:* I am excited about earning a/an
   ____________________ degree/diploma.

d. *Plan of action:* Write a simple three-step plan of action to accomplish your goal:
step 1. ______________________________
step 2. ______________________________
step 3. ______________________________

e. *Decision statement:* To accomplish this goal, I am committing _____ days (how many days) a week toward making it a reality. My reward (something that you want) for accomplishing this goal is ____________________
After completing this goal, my next educational goal is:
____

2. Spiritual Goal. A person's spiritual life is a source of pure strength. It is important to have a personal relationship with God through prayer. In your spiritual life, have goals to help spread service, hope and love in the world. When people live by these moral goals, they will treat each other more humanely.

While enduring the Texas experience, the only thing that sustained me was my belief in God. I believed strongly that I would be cleared and free again. I know that it was my belief in God that was responsible for the blessings I received. Because God wants good things for his children, I believe that the wonderful co-workers, family, friends, and strangers working and praying for my vindication were a spiritual blessing.

a. Spiritual dreams: ____________________
(Write one important spiritual dream)

b. Spiritual *goal:* I will begin by (when) ____________

c. Spiritual affirmation: I am excited about ____________

d. Plan of action: Write a simple three-step plan of action to accomplish your goal:
step 1. ______________________________
step 2. ______________________________
step 3. ______________________________

e. *Decision statement:* To accomplish this goal, I am committing _____ days (how many days) a week toward making it a reality. My reward (something that you want) for accomplishing this goal is ____________________
After completing this goal, my next spiritual goal is:
____

3. **Family Goal.** Most people love their families, they like being around them, and they are committed to them. When a couple marries, the couple become as one. They do things that are good for the couple. When the wife gives birth to a child, this birth becomes a blessing and a gift from God. This child did not come into existence until a man and woman consummated the union of their love. The child is now in their custody and their role is to teach the child the righteous ways of God. Since a child is a blessing, it is the parents' obligation to protect the child from harm physically, psychologically and spiritually, so that he or she can begin to live a righteous life.

Your ancestors have existed for thousands of years. They have survived because they have started families. Your family is probably the most important group of people to you. Getting along well with family members is important. You must try to cultivate an even better relationship. What's important is that you begin to recognize their importance to you.

If relationships with your loved ones need to be mended, let it start with you. Now is the time to do it. Do it while your loved ones are alive and well. Let the rest of your life with them be pleasurable. Find time to thank them for the hard work they have done for you. Say the magic words to your family members, "I love you!"

a. Family dreams: ______________________________
(Write one important family dream.)

b. Family *goal:* I will ______________________________
by (when) ______________________________

c. Family *affirmation:* I am excited about
____

d. *Plan of action:* Write a simple three-step plan of action to accomplish your goal:
step 1. ______________________________
step 2. ______________________________
step 3. ______________________________

e. *Decision statement:* To accomplish this goal, I am committing _____ days (how many days) a week toward making it a reality. My reward (something that you want) for accomplishing this goal is ______________
After completing this goal, my next family goal is:
____

4. Income and Work Goal. Gainful work is important. People's work is the way they earn a living. When people live a productive life, others notice the quality of their work and will want to use their services more. As an entrepreneur or an employee, give the client or company one hundred and one percent of your effort. If you are willing to go the extra mile with the additional one percent, your skills or services will be in demand because of your positive attitude and your ability to perform. You will find that your income will increase also.

People who will not work have found a reason to justify living in their current conditions. They have not found a desire strong enough to be empowered by their dreams. They spend too much time thinking about their miseries and not enough time thinking about improving their income and working on their dreams.

When you work and generate income with a purpose to serve, your conditions will begin to change for the better. *Psycho-cultivation* teaches you to work toward fulfilling your purpose to serve.

As I mentioned earlier, giving an extra one percent will ensure a measure of success in any work that is encountered. The desire and dedication of entrepreneurs are transformed into money because they take the initiative to improve themselves by meeting the needs of customers and providing quality goods and services.

a. Income-Work dreams: ______________________

(Write one important income-work dream.)

b. Income-Work *goal:* I will ______________________

by (when) ______________________

c. Income-work *affirmation:* I am excited about ________

d. *Plan of action:* Write a simple three-step plan of action to accomplish your goal:

step 1. ______________________

step 2. ______________________

step 3. ______________________

e. *Decision statement:* To accomplish this goal, I am committing _____ days (how many days) a week toward making it a reality. My reward (something that you want) for accomplishing this goal is ______________________

After completing this goal, my next career goal is:

____

5. **Career and Business Goal.** To pursue a career and to become successful, are exercises in achieving. It requires a great deal of commitment, focus and belief to make the dream of a career or business a reality. Some will try persuasion to enlist you in their business ventures thus creating difficulty in pursuing your career path. But, it can be done. All that is needed is to pursue your career path is to invest in personal development and to believe that the work you are doing is important.

There will be competing goals from other people to help them fulfill their goals and dreams. Unless you need the experience or it is economically necessary, you should follow your dreams. If your dream is starting your own business and you have done your business plan and marketing study and everything points to doing it, then go for it! This approach may be the best route although the timing may be off. A small setback may cause you to have to gain experience or raise adequate capital to fund your business or career ventures.

An effective way to diversify your income is to work in a cooperative venture where everybody's risks are minimal. In the cooperative venture commonly called networking, companies like the Amway business opportunity have been the financial answer for many families around the world. Profits can be maximized by providing products or services in this cooperative venture. The cash layout is minimal and the effort is shared by many people. Quality network marketing companies have proven to be an excellent career for many.

a. Career dreams: ______________________________

(Write one important career dream.)

b. Career *goal:* I will ______________________________
by (when) ______________________________

c. Career *affirmation:* I am excited about ____________

d. *Plan of action:* Write a simple three-step plan of action to accomplish your goal:
step 1. ______________________________
step 2. ______________________________
step 3. ______________________________

e. *Decision statement:* To accomplish this goal, I am committing _____ days (how many days) a week toward making it a reality. My reward (something that you want) for accomplishing this goal is ____________________
After completing this goal, my next career goal is:
____

6. <u>Health Goal.</u> Think for a moment about your health. How much do you value your health? If you own the wealth of the world and have poor health, the wealth is of no use to you. Poor health robs by depriving you of the pleasures to be gained from your wealth. Most people exert great effort to enjoy the material fruits of their labor. Material things can't be taken with you after you are dead; therefore, you should maintain balance in all areas of life. When it comes to your health, it goes without saying that you should exercise and eat well in order to live a long life.

Exercise can improve the quality of your life. It is hailed as being an excellent deterrent to heart disease, stress and other health challenges. We don't just want to exist in the world, we want our bodies to be healthy. The foods we eat have a profound effect on our health. Reducing fat intake, eating smaller portions of meat and increasing the intake of fruits, vegetables, whole wheat bread and others will help keep the body healthy.

a. Health dreams: ______________________________
(Write one important health dream.)
b. Health *goal:* I will ____________________________
by (when) _________________________________
c. Health *affirmation:* I am excited about
____
d. *Plan of action:* Write a simple three-step plan of action to accomplish your goal:
step 1. ________________________________
step 2. ________________________________
step 3. ________________________________

e. *Decision statement:* To accomplish this goal, I am committing _____ days (how many days) a week toward making it a reality. My reward (something that you want) for accomplishing this goal is ________________ After completing this goal, my next health goal is:

____

7. **Recreational Goal.** When your work is finished on the job, it is time to partake in some recreational activities. Many people find pleasure in running, camping, hunting, reading or walking the beaches; I do also. The gifts that recreation brings such as laughter, joy, and friendship occur so they can be shared with our friends and loved ones. Some like to sun bathe, others like to ice ski or water ski, while others like to travel. It is important to do those things which are refreshing. What is important is to be able to relax the body and mind and to be able to restart when necessary. Rejuvenation is an excellent refresher after long stretches of working on a stressful job. A change of scene is what works well for many. The goal of recreation is to refresh the individual's spirit, body and mind. I enjoy periods of reflection. Reflection is done to clear the mind from tension, confusion and disappointment. It is a time to reflect, and to evaluate your efforts, successes and failures. Everyone should set aside periods of time each week to reflect, to meditate and to calm the mind. An outcome of reflection is self-analysis. Self-analysis is reviewing yourself physically, intellectually and in other ways to learn what is needed and to formulate a plan to satisfy those needs.

a. Recreational dreams: __________________________

(Write one important recreational dream.)

b. Recreational *goal:* I will __________________________
by (when) ____________________________________

c. Recreation *affirmation*: I am excited about

____

d. *Plan of action*: Write a simple three-step plan of action to accomplish your goal:

step 1. ______________________________________
step 2. ______________________________________
step 3. ______________________________________

e. *Decision statement*: To accomplish this goal, I am committing _____ days (how many days) a week toward making it a reality. My reward (something that you want) for accomplishing this goal is:________________
After completing this goal, my next recreational goal is:
____

8. <u>Volunteer Goal</u>. The motivating force behind volunteering is to serve others. When people are giving their personal time, assistance or guidance, they are serving. There is power in the words, "Thank you for caring," coming from someone who has been served. I get a good, feeling each time I am able to help someone or to volunteer without thought of compensation. When helping others, it seems that support always comes back when it is needed most.

People have their reasons for doing for others. However, I feel that we humans have a sacred connection to all that God has created. We are responsible for each other. We are stewards of God's word. We are assigned to serve, love, respect, edify and maintain His creation. We are to use His creation but not abuse it. I think when we volunteer ourselves we are showing respect for God's creation and thus honoring our assignment. Many who are blessed with wealth should enable others to gain wealth with work and effort. While others who can give time and effort should do so.

a. Volunteer dreams: ____________________________
(Write one important volunteer dream.)
b. Volunteer *goal:* I will ___________________________
by (when) ____________________________________
c. Volunteer *affirmation:* I am excited about ___________
d. *Plan of action:* Write a simple three-step plan of action to accomplish your goal:
step 1. ______________________________________
step 2. ______________________________________
step 3. ______________________________________

e. *Decision statement:* To accomplish this goal, I am committing _____ days (how many days) a week toward making it a reality. My reward (something that you want) for accomplishing this goal is: ____________________
After completing this goal, my next volunteer goal is:
____

Read, reflect and visualize each goal daily and mentally picture yourself having already accomplished the desires you are seeking. The price of time, money or effort must be paid by you in order to be rewarded with the goal.

Affirm Your Goals

Affirmations are positive statements that are verbalized and visualized (involving all five senses in the visualization process if possible) for the purpose of influencing the mind to change or conform to suggestions. Affirmations are not practiced solely to obtain material things. Often affirmations are recited for personal development or self-image building. Affirmations are to be memorized and said morning, noon, and night. You should visualize how it would be if you had already accomplished the goal.

Some of my favorite affirmations when I was a student were as follows: "If it is in a book I can learn it." "If someone else can do it, I can do it." "If it can be done, I will never quit until it is done." When I learned more about affirmations later as an adult, I used similar ones to buildup my self-image, such as these: " I'm a winner!" "I can do anything I set my mind to do!" "I believe in myself!" "Quitters never win and winners never quit!" I am created in God's image, and I'm proud of who I am!"

When you build a house, you go to the site to ensure that the contractor is building according to the plan. It is the same as it is with a dream. Because as often as you envision the dream-construction-site mentally, it becomes a scenario which is analogous to visiting the site to reinforce and follow through on your plan. You must affirm a desire regularly when you are at your lowest point emotionally, economically, and attitudinally. By concentrating on your goal emotionally, you put action to your belief that the thing you want to obtain or improve upon is the focus of your faith. Faith is the contractor working to support your dreams. Affirmation is your visiting the mental site often to make sure it is being done according to your desires.

Step Two:
Pay the Price and Accomplish Goals

Deciding to pay the price

Every accomplishment demands that a price be paid. There is always someone who steps forward and makes a decision to pay that price. Commitment flows from a decision. Affirmation fortifies a decision. A decision must be affirmed often during the day. Through repetition, the subconscious mind begins to believe that the dream is worth the price it takes to possess it.

Fear is preventing people from receiving their dreams. Someone said that fear is, "false evidence appearing real." Early in my career in outdoor sales, I was struck with fear when making telephone calls to potential clients. I felt that it was difficult to control the process. I believed it was easy for the customer to dismiss me over the telephone by hanging up. I took it personally. I felt that what I was marketing was really the best and it would be good for my potential customers, so I regretted getting so many "no's." It took me several years to rid myself of the negative thought pictures concerning "cold calling" over the telephone. Strangely, I had no problem with "cold calling" in person, which was showing up unannounced at business locations to introduce my products.

I changed my thought pictures as far as rejections are concerned. I called on businesses, but I learned that none of them were rejecting me. It was the product they were rejecting. Some were satisfied with the product they already had, which, in some instances, had just been recently purchased. Sometimes they liked the product, but did not have any money and were too proud to let me know it.

The sales companies I worked for taught me valuable techniques to handle most of the objections in setting up appointments over the telephone. Success came when I would follow their system. The whole game of success requires that you be willing to pay the price by playing by the rules of that game. A major part of success in sales is a willingness to go through enough numbers to find the people who are willing to do business *now*.

It is definitely a numbers game. Paying the price in sales is making a critical predetermined number of telephone calls, return calls, demonstrations, and "cold calls." The sales process gave me good experience in dealing with people, overcoming my fears, and being in control of my destiny.

Taking Action

Action is a mental decision to do something which is eventually manifested in the physical world by the results from that decision. When you act on a goal, you demonstrate that you are orchestrating your efforts to achieve a predetermined result. Whenever action is required to accomplish a goal, invariably emotions are involved. I mentioned that calling potential clients to get them to buy my product was once difficult. Fear was the emotion that created the work stoppage to my success. So in order for me to take action, I had to muster up enough courage to face the fear that once held me back. I had to get my negative imagination to become a smaller factor to me than my will power. I'm now in my own business, and I am now able to call on potential clients on the telephone. To be successful on the telephone, I changed the negative emotions associated with the thought pictures when making telephone calls. I used affirmations, and I took action.

Taking action is proof that a decision has been made. President Abraham Lincoln took action to save the Union and then he freed the African slave survivors. Dr. Martin Luther King, Jr., Rosa Parks and others, also, took action to bring about the civil rights for African-Americans and all who were disenfranchised. In both cases, regrettably, these men's heroic actions cost them their lives. The consequences for your action today, in most cases, will not cost you your life. Your consequences today will probably only cost you time, money or effort.

Accomplishing The Goal

Accomplishing goals is the sweet reward of your efforts, labor, time, money and concentration of mental energy. Making it happen is a step-by-step process leading up to the accomplishment of a big dream. This climbing to the top for your dream is similar to climbing a ladder and rising higher each rung. In this illustration, the accomplishment of goals represents the rungs of a ladder. At the completion of each rung—the goal—there needs to be a reward.

Step Three:
Continue The Journey with New Goals and Dreams

If you experience no set backs at the completion of your goal attempts, move forward by continuing the journey with new goals. I am aware that there will be setbacks on the road to achieving your dreams and goals. I have experienced a multitude of setbacks with goals that I have pursued. However, the one thing I did not do is quit the pursuit of these goals. If the goals remain sound to you over time, just continue to reset the goal until you have succeeded.

When you experience setbacks, first do some self analysis to see what went wrong. Look for the real reason(s) why you have not succeeded. Sometimes when you uncover the real reason, the solution may require that you change or leave your comfort zone and expose yourself to scrutiny. If you really want to succeed at accomplishing goals, you need to leave the comfort zone and just do it!

Second, if the goal is something material, create vivid thought pictures of yourself with the goal. Imagine yourself smelling the goal or being in the environment in which the goal exists. Imagine the sounds in the environment or the sounds of the actual goal. Feel the texture of the goal or feel the excitement associated with possessing the goal. Picture the colors of the goal. Imagine yourself tasting or eating your favorite foods in the presence of the goal.

Third, get proper training or education so that you have the qualifications to acquire, realistically, the goal. If you are not ready to possess the goal, then often the goal will not become yours.

Fourth, if you require improvements in your self-image, isolate the weaknesses. Then, take the weaknesses and turn them into positive affirmations. Before I changed my thought pictures in sales, I visualized people saying "no" to me on my sales calls. I changed this visual thought picture to customers saying "yes" to my calls. I made positive affirmations to rescript the negative thought pictures in my sales experience. In my new affirmations, I picture thoughts of customers saying "yes" to me and they were glad I called on them. This technique will not change your habit right away; it may take saying the affirmation hundreds of times over a period of time.

After accomplishing a goal, your journey should continue with a new dream that's transformed into a goal. Once you have developed a plan of action to accomplish the goal—there's no stopping you! Keep in mind that the dream is the focus. The reward will cause you to press forward with power in the face of all adversity so that you may win in the end.

Let God Sustain Your Faith

"Let God sustain your faith" is one of my favorite quotes because it happens to be what works for me. In addition, I believe that God's word is a moral lens through which people should view the world and by which they behave. His word addresses all moral and social ills. A belief in God and the Scriptures helped to answer all of my questions. I became stronger as a result of my beliefs. To have my beliefs come true was extra special.

When I was in pain for answers, suffering for positive conversation, hurting for freedom from bondage, working to clear my name, and missing my family, friends, loved ones, and career, God heard my prayers! My prayers were answered!

Set New Goals

Have you ever planned a trip to a distant city? If you have, you would probably remember the many towns and cities along the way. There were rest areas to stop to refresh yourself. Every time you exited to rest, you may have gotten something to eat, drink or you may have just walked around. In making plans to acquire your dreams, they, too, must be planned thoroughly. Using the above illustration, your dream represents the destination—the distant city you want to get to. If the dream is what you are after, keep focusing on it. Take advantage of the goals because they keep you in touch with the dream. Every time you exit to pursue your goals, remember you are taking a temporary break to refresh yourself because the dream is what you are after.

When you are in the proximity of your dream destination, set new goals into motion. Start the planning process again. You must decide whether you are going to stay, return, or move on to the next dream. The important thing to remember is that when you successfully reach the distant city—the dream—it does not end your journey. You can do something else. You can grow and expand, but you must move on because stagnation leads to the death of initiative.

PART 4

Attitude for Success # 3:

Linking Personal Growth to Prosperity

Personal Growth

The third stage, the growth phase of the tomato seed, occurs throughout the life of the plant. The plant continues to grow, with the cells duplicating themselves over and over, cell by cell. As the plant penetrates the surface of the ground, there is rapid plant growth and a great deal of struggle. Once it is above the ground, it has to contend with the elements of nature, man, birds, animals or weeds. Yet, the plant succeeds. All of these situations do not deter the plant from pursuing its destiny—its genetic predestination which is to "be fruitful and multiply."

Unlike the tomato plant, many people give-up the struggle and stop learning or improving themselves in the face of a few adversities. It's been said, "If you can believe it, you can achieve it." So keep on believing, keep on struggling, and keep on learning and improving. You have what it takes to make it, for if you can dream it, that's proof you can achieve it. All you need to do is work and focus on this process and the dream will become a reality.

CHAPTER 6

Beginning Prosperity with Personal Growth and Improvement

Understanding Personal Growth

Two of the most misunderstood lessons of success are growth and struggle. As you will see later, life has its struggles waiting for you to break through to a higher level of success. Not everyone understands that dreams are part of the vision which comes first, then the struggle, then the victorious fulfillment of the dream. The cycle continues with another dream, another struggle, the victorious fulfillment of a dream, etc.

Personal skills and growth are some of the jewels that you have to offer. Society wants to know the answer to this question: What can you do or what goods can you produce or what service do you have to offer? As a professional, or skilled technician, you must be able to translate your skills into profit for the corporation, or be willing to learn on the job the skills necessary to earn a respectable income.

In everything that you do, you must be willing to improve yourself. That is growth. You must be willing to learn new things. That is growth. Life wants you to grow, expand, be more, do more and become more. When you introduce growth into your life, you will be in demand for your services.

If you are good at what you do, the market will pay whatever price you demand for your service. You can't expect to waste your days and time away on selfish indulgences and expect to be paid. No, it does not work that way. We are here to serve. Anyone who is not growing and improving does not intend to be of benefit to the community. It is through our skills and talents we are able to serve and contribute to the community.

Your relationship to society is established based on serving and doing something to help yourself and others. Crime occurs because an individual has become selfish and self-serving. Self-serving persons are benefiting themselves. Success comes when you work within in the law, and you serve others in a positive way. Serving others is the main ingredient. In a relationship regarding society or family, you have to sever all relationships which prevent you from contributing to society and the family. Society, for the most part, is moving in unison toward one path, a path leading to wealth, freedom, justice and equality.

When we see someone, one of the first things we do is to size the person up based on our values. If you happen to be an employer, you want to determine whether the individual fits in your corporate environment. If the employer is looking for people who can make shapes such as stars, circles, and rectangles and you can only make squares, then you will not get the job. Whenever you are employed, you are being employed because you have the skills and proper attitude to perform your duties. You have to fit into the corporate culture and buy into the corporate mission. During the interviewing process, employers take notice of the interviewee. They get a first impression, then they look for commonality, such as his or her ability to perform the job activity, and ability to communicate effectively. Additionally, employers examine his or her work history, educational achievement and community involvement. The employer is wanting to determine, in a brief period during the interviewing process, how well your skills, training and values will blend with the corporate culture.

Grooming is an important factor for success because it creates a good first impression of how highly you value yourself. Your body is beautiful, unique and personal. This is why your body is separated physically from everyone else's body.

It is difficult to respect seriously a person whose attire is inappropriate i.e. dresses too short, trousers hanging below the waist, etc. Granted, some are trying to get the most out of the shock response, but a future employer or the banker who might consider lending you money or employing you one day may be watching. Whether you are conscious or unconscious of how you come to dress the way you do, the attire of those in the fashion industry and the music world establish the norm for dressing. This reminds me of the king in the story "The Emperor's New Clothes." The king was tricked into paying a huge sum of money to clothes designers to create a beautiful costume for an important event. They fooled the king into thinking that they had woven him the finest clothes ever and he had to be sophisticated to notice it; but instead, he was wearing nothing at all. Except for a little boy, none including the wise men in the kingdom wanted to seem unsophisticated, so the kings' advisors did not tell the king he was unclothed. A lesson to learn is that fashion designers or those in the music industry may be manipulating young impressionable minds to purchase their creations because it is profitable for them. Are they stuffing their pockets and in the end you become a social misfit, "a poster child", a buffoon or a "fashion statement" of their creation? Sometimes, you have to stop and think whether your attire is appropriate for the venue. It is easy to tell whether your attire is appropriate—just look at the attire of others around you and if your attire is "off the scale" for what is normal, then you need to make an adjustment. There will be a time and a place to properly express your individuality.

Life Skills for Successful Living

Your life skills assist you in your interactions with people. We have to work with people, and how we treat them is reflected in our level of life skills which reveal how much respect we have for others. Improved life skills will help you better understand the power and potential to be a productive force in the community and the society in which you live.

The general focus of life skills is placed on helping people to develop coping skills, problem solving skills, reasoning and positive thinking skills which are needed to activate a mental attitude and properly meet challenges or confrontations in their lives. Positive outcomes will arise when you learn what strategies give you the most effective results. When you are comfortable with these skills, you will be able to handle a multitude of life's challenges.

To improve reasoning skills, young people need to learn how to break up and assess problems and difficulties by having a clear focus on their values, goals and aspirations. This will reveal their strengths and weaknesses and will help to fertilize and enrich their potential for positive change. Good reasoning skills will help youngsters see obstacles or difficulties as positives that *motivate* and not *hinder* mental growth and development.

The accent is on the power of positive thinking and understanding the effect it has on the empowerment of people to affect change, achievement, and success in their lives. The key focus is on viewing the foundation for achievement and success as forces not outside ourselves, but inborn. If we know how to use our innate abilities to unlock the door to our possibilities and potentials, we will achieve success. Life skills are essential in meeting the demands of life which requires flexibility, and teamwork.

Having the ability to conceive dreams and to be willing to act on those dreams is having dream skills. When you are constantly dreaming about your future and acting on those dreams, one door of opportunity may close but another door will open for you. In the past years, there have been a number of post office fatalities caused by former employees. Most of them were upset because they had lost their employment. The disgruntled employees took guns and went in and shot some employees at the post office. I believe if people are shown other ways to realize their dreams while working their regular jobs, they may not be so quick to hurt other employees. A job can be terminated at any time. With a dream, you would be prepared for this kind of adversity by diversifying. If one is ever fired, the termination would not devastate his or her family, because you have another monetary source which is generating enough income to help absorb the shock of being laid off or terminated.

A dream is a positive thing that you want in life. It exists in your mind first; it moves you forward if you act on it. The dream takes your mind off your current circumstances. Your thoughts are focused on the future, the dream. You will begin to do the proactive things required to change, such as talking to experts, getting more knowledge, and visiting the dream mentally or physically.

When you have a positive attitude you believe that what you want in life will happen. You don't doubt that a future dream home, an invention, a college degree, the promotion or business venture will come true. You know that they will come true. With a positive attitude, you will achieve success. To become positive, you have to think positively. Achievement aids positive thinking. It is realizing that you can't alternate between positive attitudes and negative attitudes in life and still get what you want. You have to claim and believe the dream is yours and do the work that is necessary to make it a reality.

The following are but a few crucial life skills which are essential in being successful in society:

First, problem solving skills involve being able to break up into pieces all parts of a problem—first to understand it and second to overcome it. Once you understand how the pieces of the problem fit together, you are better able to see the big picture. The components you are looking to discover in the problem is the cause and effect relationship. Understanding these components will unify the fragments and help to solve the problem. Once the cause is known, it might just involve getting help, getting more knowledge, earning more money or asking for more time. "If it is a human problem, it has a human solution."

Second, reasoning skills give you the ability to assess problems and difficulties to derive at the best solution. Good reasoning skills involve using a solution pathway to get to your desired conditions. It's using the best case scenarios to get the effect that you desire.

I enjoy a good game of chess even though I know that my reasoning skills are being challenged by my opponent's skills. The moves I make cause my opponent to respond with a move he or she hopes will weaken my strategy. If my opponent does manage to weaken my current strategy, I will not quit. Instead, I will use improved reasoning to think ahead three or four moves in advance while considering his best counter moves. If you can learn to think through adversities based on sound reasoning, you can become successful at home, in the workplace, and in society. In order to do this you have to ask yourself this question time and time again, "What is the best way to handle this problem without anyone getting hurt in the process?"

Third, coping skills are desired as a way to deal with new and unfamiliar situations. The best way to cultivate a coping skill attitude is to learn from people you trust and in whom you confide. Ask these individuals how they would handle your current situation. Make sure that the people to whom you are listening are generally able to achieve good outcomes. The military trains its soldiers how to cope while living in the wilderness if they are separated from their unit. They learn which plants and bugs are safe to eat or where a good source of drinking water can be found. All these coping skills are taught to help increase the soldier's survivability. When working to encourage greater coping skills in others, you must believe in that person, teach, encourage independence, and have faith in his or her ability and competence to do well in life. When you learn improved coping skills, others will be able to learn from your experience.

Fourth, employers want employees to learn their jobs and to have good people skills. The employer wants you to be one, who gets along with other co-workers and produce quality work.

A positive attitude, and a good self-image help to put youths in the right attitude for learning and respecting authority. Having the right attitude for learning is just as important as earning a quality education. Education means having specific intellectual tools for tasks required to support the various vital roles of society. In addition to earning a degree from a four-year institutional, the youth can acquire a quality education from a junior college or technical college. With education as a tool and a good attitude as fuel, in life, everybody can be pulled up another level plus some.

A tool must have a tool handler, someone to use the tool. Education is that tool which allows you to make better use of your ability and even develop other skills. Education enables an individual's inborn ability to learn and become teachable, so as to better utilize his or her resources. In an increasingly advancing technological and computerized era, more knowledge and skills are needed. A positive attitude and self-image can help to put a youth in the right attitude for learning and respecting authority. Quality education and a good attitude can become instruments for success.

Educating for Moral and Economic Success

When I was a child my mother influenced me to get a college education. Her reasoning was that a good education would help me meet life's challenges. She wanted all of her children to experience the success a quality education could provide. My mother knew that I could not depend on my father because at that time he was not a part of my life. It would be over two decades before I would meet my father and spend some time with him.

My mother was right. Now I realize why I would need an education. Though my stepfather was very generous to me, it was not his obligation to educate me and meet my financial needs. It was my biological father, mother and my responsibility to ensure that I get a college education. In addition to receiving assistance from grants, my mother assisted financially with my college debts. I worked during my college years, often studying late into the night in order to stay abreast.

I view education as a two-part process: Part one is to build a positive attitude, a positive self-esteem and a positive self-image in people. Part two is to earn a quality education. A positive attitude is like fuel; it gets you going and it supplies the motivation. Children are with their parent or parents for the first six years of their lives; they are not in school most of the day. It is the parents grand opportunity to build their children's attitude, self-esteem and self-image. With a positive attitude and self-image, children will have confidence in themselves and will be ready for school and life. In the formative years, a positive attitude is as important to a youth's preparation to enter school as high school academics is to higher education.

Self-image

Your present self-image is cultivated from a number of sources including yourself, peers, family environment and national attitude. Learning to improve your self-image is important for success. Although, you may have to struggle somewhat, you can experience success. To grow in all areas of your life, you must eliminate all negativism hindering you from creating a positive mental attitude. A positive mental attitude is developed by having positive thought pictures of prosperity and success.

You may have heard the old adage, "Birds of a feather flock together." You will not see an eagle and a raven flying together. Birds that are dissimilar usually don't share similar interests just as people who are successful, usually, don't surround themselves on a regular basis with unsuccessful people. It is one's thoughts that people are attracted to. Another way of looking at it is people with a positive attitude usually seek out other people whose attitudes are positive. Successful people will not seek advice on success from people with an "attitude of poverty." It isn't because they are better; it's because they have conditioned their minds only for success-oriented messages.

The minds of success-conscious people are disciplined to produce and achieve. These winners succeed because of resources such as education, skills, mentors, self-help material, and a desire to grow and improve. They have discovered that in order to enrich themselves and their families, they must provide goods and services that will benefit hundreds or thousands of people. Their success is based on discovering the public's demand and meeting that demand with a quality product or service.

A negative self-image is often associated with an attitude of poverty. This attitude produces negative thought pictures which often lead to crime, lack of desire and lack of belief in one's self. This thinking is the basis or cause of many of life's undesirable circumstances. Negative thinking breeds an attitude of poverty which is cultivated by watching life take place instead of being willing to participate in the arena of life. Your current thinking has attracted the circumstances and conditions that now exist in your life.

The destiny of people is decided by their decision to manage the input of thought pictures entering their minds. To change a negative thought picture, all you need to do is substitute it with a positive thought. The thoughts that constitute your mental makeup all contribute to your present self-image, just as the cells of the body make up your physical self-image.

The self-image is how you view yourself in your imagination. Your opinion of your image, whether viewed positively or negatively, is what's real to you. Look at yourself in the mirror! What you are looking at is a unique and wonderful person! Even if you had twin brothers or sisters, their attitudes and thoughts would not be like yours. As a twin, your physical image can be a duplicate, but the self-image is different and it differs from person to person.

It is interesting that the physical body can be hurt. However, the intangible part of you that makes you aware, some call it the soul or intellect, can't be physically hurt. The self-image is the focus of my concern. The intangible self-image and attitude, can be influenced emotionally. These emotions affect how you imagine yourself to be. The self-image is protective, and it will cause you to avoid pain to protect you.

At first glance, an unshaven man, smelly, and needing a haircut, might appear to have a poor self-image. Or perhaps the clothes and appearance could suggest that he has just come off a hunting trip. The attitude is the first indicator of whether this person has a good self-image—not his or her clothes. The clothes however, help make a first impression. In addition, the manner in which people maintain their hygiene and appearance over a period of time is a better indicator of how they feel about themselves.

The input and the messages you react to from people, affect your attitude, emotion, and action. To make sure you are on target with your agenda, you must have positive dreams, virtues and principles. If you allow your self-image to become unbalanced or upset over a minor concern, you end up with an unsettled self-image concerning that subject. If your self-image is adversely affected a number of times, this will erode your general self-confidence which contributes toward a poor self-image.

CHAPTER 7

Developing Thoughts and Improving Self-image

Shielding a Child's Self-image From Unwarranted Harm

Your present self-image is cultivated from a number of sources including yourself, peers, family environment and national attitude. Learning to improve your self-image is important for success. Although you may have to struggle somewhat, you can experience success. To grow in all areas of your life, eliminate all negativism hindering you from creating a positive mental attitude. A positive mental attitude is developed by having positive thought pictures of prosperity and success.

The subconscious mind stores information from all sources. The subconscious is like a video camera which records impressions of sounds and thought pictures. A lot of today's weird behavior and dispassionate crimes are a result of people who were overexposed to vice. Many of these acts of violence are a result of being pre-exposed to drugs, sex and violence. These experiences are stored in the subconscious mind. Someone may feel inclined to act-out a deed which was never experienced before. The deed stemmed from a thought picture from an unexperienced source "planted" in the subconscious mind from pre-exposed sources.

Today, a child does not have to live in poverty or a ghetto to experience the unwanted influence of drugs and violence. Parents are allowing drugs and violence to go unchallenged in their living rooms, thanks to the television and other sources. The key is for parents to control the unfavorable and undesired input being fed into the minds of children. The suggestions below are designed to start at age eight months and continue through age eighteen. From age twelve until the youth leaves the home, there should be teachings which include spirituality, educational and athletic activities, structured living, chores and accountability as substitutes to reduce television viewing.

CHARACTER BENCHMARK: LESSON # 3

Controlling Undesirable Information

You can control the unfavorable and undesirable input by trying the following with your children:

- taking control of your home in the early stages of your children's lives;
- attending their schools;
- attending religious services;
- becoming better acquainted with their peers;
- living in the best possible neighborhood you can afford;
- having non-challenging conversations with them on topics of their interest;
- limiting their television time and program content;
- screening what they listen to on the radio; and
- saying "no" to outrageously expensive clothes which are often requested by youngsters.

You are under your children's influence when you allow them to get you to meet their outrageous demands. Instead, offer to buy reasonably priced articles to wear. If these things are not wanted, help your children to find a part-time job so they can save money to purchase their expensive clothes when they are old enough to be on their own. Don't allow your children to bring anything into your house if you cannot account for where it came.

Thought Reflections in Others

When you rear children in your household, you have an important task. What you tell children will be reflected in their lives. The part of a child's life that is most affected is his or her self-image. The self-image is that invisible part of a person's imagination that is not considered much by adults when rearing a child. As an example, if you throw paper in a basket it becomes a waste basket. If you throw loose change in the basket it becomes a loose change basket. Using the waste paper scenario, when you speak negatively about children with whom you have emotional bonds, it contributes to inhibiting or tearing down their vulnerable self-images. If, on the other hand, you encourage children to believe in themselves, their self-image will be positive. By doing this, you help to buildup the children's self-confidence, and they become self-assured.

When rearing children, it is significant to consider helping to improve their self-image. The self-image is not tangible. It defines how they view themselves or what they feel they can or can not do. People have a complex self-image; it indicates what kinds of things they allow themselves to achieve or what kinds of things they are capable of doing. Sometimes a person's self-image will indicate a personal assessment of a situation, which may not be accurate about the person's abilities. Conditioning themselves to believe these things, it takes change to realize new dreams or abilities. The capacity to change their self-image into self-assured and productive people rests solely with them.

Society, peers, family and the individual all contribute to whether the individual will have a self-image that will be appropriate in society. The individual has the biggest influence on how his or her self-image will evolve. When society attempts to decide an individual's appropriateness, the result ends up being biased. The result is biased because society has to make a comparison and the comparison does not include a person's true potential.

It takes healthy cells to produce a healthy body. It takes healthy thought pictures to produce a healthy self-image. While a child is young, it is important to protect him or her from detractors to the self-image. At every opportunity, there should be teaching in a child's life as a defense against detractors. Foul language, negative "put-downs" and negative values weaken the self-image.

Developing the Self-image of a Wise King's Son

The following tale of a wise king gives insight into the value of encouraging the self-image of others to grow, develop and mature. On the continent of Africa, deep within the interior, lived a wise man called King Marzinza. As a youth, King Marzinza was noted for his wisdom. His wise story telling was so highly regarded that kings, queens and noblemen from distant lands would travel great distances just to confer with him and to hear his wise tales.

On one cool, bright day, many people came to hear the King's once-a-month address which was open to the public. This was the time when everyone outside of the tribal family as well as the members of the tribe were invited to sit and hear the wise tales of King Marzinza. The crowd waited patiently for the moment King Marzinza, the queen and the court of wise elders would sit before the great mass of people for the king to serve them with points of wisdom.

King Marzinza was probably a man of forty-three. He came from a dynasty of kings that stretched back in history several hundred years. He was a tall, stately and handsome man with a chocolate-colored complexion and black, curly hair. He was dressed in the finest of bright royal clothes produced by the citizens of his tribe. The country's climate seemed like paradise, and the King's clothes were designed to fit him accordingly.

King Marzinza earned his wisdom because of his willingness to put himself in a position to learn by seeking wisdom. When his father, the late king of the tribe, spoke, his son Marzinza was always there listening. Marzinza was better known for his listening skills rather than his speaking skills. When he was required to speak, few in the kingdom recognized his voice. He not only listened to the wisdom of his father, the king, but he listened to his mother, the queen, grandparents, wise men and members of the tribe as well. All of the information that he learned would pay off in the future because he had to preside over many difficult assemblies.

Approaching the gathering was the king and queen flanked by the court of wise elders in the great clearing under a huge, green tree. The day was beautiful and accented by a completely blue, cloudless sky. The sounds of animals running could be heard faintly in the background. The birds were chirping lovely sounds while monkeys gave chase. The monkeys' vocals gradually faded away as they distanced themselves from the gathering. The colorful array of beautiful flowers all growing among each other appeared to be a planned bouquet. The tall, green palm trees blocked nearly half of the heat from the sun, making the gathering site cool and appropriately comfortable. The water from the nearby river had a calming effect for everyone there.

The crowd settled down to a still quietness as King Marzinza seated himself in a special chair called the Royal Chair of the People. Every tribal leader contributed a piece of wood or fabric for the chair's construction. The chair was regarded as the King's seat of power and respect. The king started into his story without hesitation.

This story is about how a wise family developed the leadership and self-image of their only son. Everyone in the crowd wondered how the great king could develop a story from such an obvious subject. He started, "It takes the sunlight a little more than a few minutes to leave the sun and travel to earth. The wonderful rays of sunlight which reach the earth do not keep the planet waiting long for heat and light to brighten our paths and fields. Our country benefits in a multitude of ways from the sun's light, but among the many benefits of sunlight is its price, free of charge to the rich and the poor. Plants, animals, friends and even our enemies depend on the sun for life. The sun creates the proper temperature-balanced environment for all of God's creations to thrive and prosper. In fact, the sun has been serving this planet faithfully for billions of years."

The king said parents are the custodians of children. When you think of your relationship to your child, think of yourself as the sun. The light from the sun promotes life and the sun's gravity holds the planets in its influence as gravity holds us to the earth. Gravity represents parental actions, habits, virtues, values and principles to which children are exposed and shape their character. Think of your child as the earth. The earth depends on the sun for warmth, for its orbital path and for promotion of life on earth.

We all need sun to live so that everything can "be fruitful and multiply." When you are upset, think of the effect that your words have on your child. The sole purpose of your words to your child should be to love, discipline, encourage, correct, instruct or build-up. Never call your child stupid, crazy, ugly, dumb, a quitter, a loser or use statements such as: "You will never become anything," or "You are going to end up dead or in prison." Do you want your words when angry, upset or indifferent to be reflected in his or her life? No, I should think not, so begin to see your positive words as giving life and absorbing that life when your child listens to them.

As parents, just as the sun's light benefits the earth, imagine your words as individual rays of sunlight, each having a beneficial purpose when heard by your child. Whenever you say positive, encouraging words to children, the words will build or improve their self-image. Their self-image will absorb and reflect to others your words and attitude as warm, loving and edifying. Your children will live life accordingly. Conversely, when you say negative things to your children, the words will tear down their self-image. They will absorb and reflect to others your negative words and attitude. These words will become negative acts of behavior. If you promote coldness, insecurity and apathy, your children will internalize this behavior.

Many years ago, in one of the tribes in this kingdom lived a very respectable family called the Ulam family. The parents of this family gave birth to a baby boy. The new parents loved the baby boy more than the vast wealth that they possessed. They wanted their child to grow up and live a righteous and successful life. When the boy grew and became of age, the parents enrolled him in one of the finest schools of learning in the country, and he did well in his courses.

Something else was very important to the Ulam family and that was the spiritual life of their son. With this in mind, the father searched the vastness of the country in search of the wisest man in all of the land. The wise man was located in a small town ninety miles from where the family lived. The family bought their son along to be enrolled in this great wise man's study group because the father believed that one's relationship with God is the cornerstone of life. The wise man agreed to teach the young man wisdom and to enhance his knowledge about God greatly.

The wise man said to the father, "I will teach the young man wisdom and the knowledge of God; however, the price may be too much for you to pay." Yet, the father was unshaken in his desire for his son to become the wise man's pupil. The father said, "Name your price!" The wise man said, "Your price will be all the wealth that you [father] possessed."

The wise man realized if the Ulam family gave up all of their wealth in exchange for their son's training, it was possible for them to replace their wealth again. He based his mode of thinking on the spiritual principle of sowing and reaping which is based on serving. Like the farmer, if you sow a crop of corn you will reap a crop of corn. You get out of life what you give to life. The wise man knew that if you developed wealth once, all that is needed is to reproduce the quality and the amount of service that made you wealthy the first time. The degree of service you render helps determine how much success you experience. Therefore, the more people you serve the wealthier you become.

The problem with the Ulam family, however, was that they inherited most of their wealth. They were excellent, though, at expanding it and managing it. If the Ulams failed to replace their wealth, then the son would surely be able to become wealthy as a result of the knowledge and wisdom he would learn. It took the father less than a minute to contemplate and absorb what he had just heard from the wise man before he agreed to his offer.

The wise man stated to the father that he would not have to hand over his entire wealth until their son finished the two-year course. Two years later, the young man completed the training. It seemed that the time could not have come and gone any quicker because the Ulam family hadn't seen their son in a while.

Just as they agreed two years earlier, the vast wealth of the Ulam family was officially transferred to the wise man. The family had a place to live after giving up their wealth because during the two years their son was in training, they managed to learn new skills, become employed and earned a modest living. They created a separate income for the family in addition to their former wealth.

The wise man left this advice with the Ulam family so that they would be able to reinforce his teachings. He said, The reason your son reflects in his life your attitude as well as the attitude of his environment is that you are nurturing and developing the abstract self-image and attitude of your son's personality. When you rear the physical son, you are careful in the foods your son eats. You never get to see his self-image as you see his physical body. The physical body cries for food, clothes and shelter, but not the self-image. Whether you realize it, you need to be careful of unproductive sources of influences and negative ideals your son comes in contact with. Healthy self-images need encouraging, edifying and self-affirming words which are free from the influence of vulgarity, sex and violence.

A person's thoughts and words can negatively influence the self-image of his listeners if those individuals are not secure. If the person is benevolent, then his or her instructions will lead others on the right path. On the other hand, the words of an evil person can corrupt others and lead them down a path of destruction.

King Marzinza stated that the parents of the son in this family never did regain their former wealth, although they did live long enough to see their son become wealthy beyond anything they could imagine. They lived to see their son marry a princess.

From that day until the present, the Ulam family has ruled the country for several centuries. I belong to that dynasty of kings that started with the Ulam family. Ulam is my family's last name and it stands for the Wise One. According to my family custom, a king must improve his self-image, character and spirituality and that of his subjects using wisdom and discernment to be qualified to govern.

Predisposition to Negative Thoughts

When parents listen to the radio or watch television programs with their children, they are often surprised with the inappropriate behavior, scenes, words and phrases used. Parents are left thinking, "I thought this program was appropriate for family viewing." The family is being predisposed to information outside of their value system that they would rather their young children not be exposed to. Television programmers and producers are usually an uncaring and an uninvolved third party whose motives are for financial gain and not love for your love ones.

In this technological era, children are predisposed to vice because of television before they are enrolled in the first grade. If, on the other hand, the television program is good for family viewing, then it's the commercials that are often not appropriate for the young child's mind. Remember, it is through pictures that we best process information. If we hear words, our minds have to convert them to pictures. Think of an object. You probably envisioned a picture of the object.

Hollywood producers and advertisers are competing for the minds of people, and they have chosen the emotions and people's curiosity about life and action outside of their environment to entice them. Also, let's face it, in all fairness to Hollywood producers, a lack of parental awareness and guidance also contributes to Hollywood television programmers' power. Television programming often glorifies killing, maiming and illicit sex which contributes to the development of a youth's self-image and his or her propensity for that reality. The ultimate burden is to be placed on the parents because they should be the "informational gate keepers" to the home. Parents should view television programs with their children and viewing should be limited.

Many parents fail to turn the television off or turn to another channel when viewing becomes inappropriate. They don't give their children an alternative input based on their values. Because of the accumulation of television viewing, possibly, the mind is exposed to information on how to kill, how to become sexually active, how to smoke, how to dress and other concepts which are mentally stored and then actualized.

Often parents have two jobs, which prevent them from spending quality time with their children. The children spend many hours in front of the television at a young age, retrieving and storing information in their minds. When you use the television as a tutor, it does not consider your virtues and beliefs when it tutors your child how to handle conflicts, behavior or get along with others.

If the allure of street life is greater than what is taught in the home, then it goes without saying that the street life will influence the children. There is hope, if children are reared "in the way they should go." There is a good chance they will return to their training. When children are taught good virtues and principles, they will grow up with the attributes you instilled. When a conflict in their virtues arise, their home training should remind them of the proper course of action to take. Instead, if they practice wrong choices, it will be difficult for them to become congruent with their values and principles. However, if they are willing, they can choose to change at any point in their lives and return to their values.

Young people's moral systems will not differentiate between what is appropriate and what is not appropriate unless their parents have worked hard to solidify their positive values *(see Appendix C for the pledge for personal change)* into the youth's memory. If the youth's moral defensive system is not in place, we can't definitively say how children categorize violence and immorality. Yet, I think they are stored and categorized in their memory as unchallenged options. If a youth's values, principles and defensive system are not yet in the moral defensive mode, the child's predisposition to television vices become a viable option for him or her to play out in real life.

I believe youth, to a large extent, and grown-ups too, are responsible for the children's actions. Parents need to be better informed to the harm negative predisposition has on children. Ideally, any exposure to undesirable knowledge should occur when their values and principles are intact in a child's life, giving him or her the ability to discern right from wrong. Most parents want their children to have a fair chance at becoming self-supporting, consenting adults and productive citizens. Controlling what children watch on television is an important step in that direction.

Environmental Thought Pictures

During the spring season, the pollen from trees and flowers is blown about by the gusty winds. Although this author is not affected by the pollen, it sometimes causes an irritating reaction in some people. Sufferers complain of headaches, runny eyes, and short temperament. The pollen happens to be the way nature propagates the species of various plant life. The pollen is a needed component of the environment for plants; however, because people are part of the environment, some are adversely affected. Sufferers can reduce the effect of pollen through medication.

People can reduce the effect of an unfavorable economic environment by changing their thought pictures. The community, state and country are part of the environment. The prevailing thoughts of that environment affect attitudes. If there is poverty in their surroundings, then poverty is the prevailing thought of the people in that environment. If people are mostly successful, success will be the prevailing thought pattern of the people in that environment. If their neighborhood is undesirable, they can transcend it. It takes changing thought pictures, and following new paths to make dreams become a reality.

Surroundings are the most effective environmental influence on anyone. Unless you are guided to think otherwise, you will begin to think that the level of achievement in your surroundings is only what you are capable of attaining. Environmental attitudes are the opinions of family members, and people regarding things, places and events. If you learned to accept only positive and useful information from your communications with other people, you will generally be positive in your interactions.

Developing a positive attitude is to a larger extent contingent on your environment, yet it helps to contribute, through your thinking, to how successful you will be in life. To become successful in life, we have to work with other people. It helps if our attitude is positive toward them. A positive attitude is having a pleasant disposition.

Thought Pictures From Self

Much of our source of knowledge, information and beliefs come from the following: the media, culture, family, peers, environment, and ourselves. These sources of information influence our view of life and contribute toward our circumstances. Positive thought is a key to helping unlock success in life. Your view of yourself is like a directional pointer, leading you in the path of your dominant thought pictures.

The most important influence to you is yourself. All sources of input (or messages) coming to you can be made benign by changing your thinking into positive thought pictures. Positive self-input helps you to have confidence to meet the challenges of life successfully. To become free from the negative influences of others, it is important to have unwavering thought pictures of yourself.

Having Control of Thoughts

Whatever value you have placed on yourself, your self-image will adjust accordingly, to accommodate it. People who feel that they are worthless have placed their value to serve and to contribute at nearly zero. These people have failed to control their thoughts. They allow their hygiene to go unattended, there is no money in their pockets and some even attempt to commit suicide. People can change their thoughts, improve their self-worth, and learn a skill. Positive thoughts change people, thereby, enabling them to make valuable contributions to society. When individuals feel that they have nothing to offer, they will not contribute. Their lives will become full of perplexing and baffling thoughts which keep them from finding a way to success.

When faced with problems or undesirable economic circumstances, some people have become victims of negative thinking. These formerly productive people have succumbed to negative thoughts about themselves and their dream. Their thoughts created an attitude of poverty. This thinking has caused some to become homeless people. However, a solution does exist for this situation. The way to control their thoughts is for them to understand the five attitudes of *psycho-cultivation*: have a spiritual purpose to serve others; maintain a positive vision or a dream to focus on; grow and increase in knowledge and skills; overcome adversity, and become productive so that the fruits of their labor enable them to overcome adversity and achieve dreams.

With a purpose, you will know that you are here to serve others. When you are working toward a goal or dream, your thoughts will cause you to be in control of your efforts. One of the purposes of a job is for you to work toward something that is important to the employer, you, and your family. That's why you feel good when you are achieving, working, or helping.

Leadership over Self

Self-leadership is taking control of the personal leadership of your life and the direction or path you have decided to take. The greatest obstacle to self-leadership is the influence of other people you care about. As a leader, you have to stop allowing others to do your thinking, especially when the direction of their leadership can potentially hurt yourself or others. You have to begin to think for yourself and take control of the leadership of your life. Start now, by saying no to things that are not in your best interest. Illegal drugs, violence, and crime are not in your best interest; they don't help you to live a responsible life.

Leaders have to be able to set themselves apart from negative influences and to continue their journey until they have succeeded in achieving their goals. Leaders realize that everyone is on a personal path to accomplish a vision. However, the leader with the greatest resolve will attract others into his or her vision.

Self-leaders are concerned with the direction their lives are taking which prevent others from determining their success or failure. Self-leaders realize the need for respecting those who provide for them. Self-leadership cannot be given to you by someone. You have to seize it, just as long as no one is hurt. You earn it by "doing the things that you know need to be done without someone having to tell you to do it."

The path to self-leadership can be achieved by exercising vision. As a leader, you will not be content with following the beaten paths of others. You will want to start your own visionary path which will lead to a brighter future and also will give you greater control and freedom. Saying "no" to people who want to lead you off your vision path is all a part of your leadership duties.

Dominant Thoughts on Display

The information that you allow to influence you will be no better than the input. If you allow antisocial thoughts to influence you, your life will be limited by society because of your actions and deeds. Society will incarcerate you as one who breaks the law.

Output behavior is a habit that you have allowed to occupy your thinking. It drives the kind of action you take. Also, it is the result of all sources of input, which forms your thinking and actions.

When I was in college, a part of my engineering course work involved programming a computer driven numerical control (N.C.) milling machine to mill a gear. The N.C. machine was designed to mill machine parts. As part of my requirements for passing the course, I had to design and fabricate a gear. I used my mechanical drawing instruments and equipment to design the gear on paper.

The machine was very sophisticated in that all I had to do was to key in a number of inputs and the mill would move from left to right, up and down, in and out at varying depths. When the machine was properly programmed, the movements seemed to operate using smooth, harmonic strokes. Then I programmed all of the gear contours into the computer. My first, second, and third attempts at programming the computer to produce a gear were basically an exercise in futility. The N.C. machine went into all kinds of weird directions, rarely touching the block of steel I clamped to the machine. Therefore, I corrected the input, by programming, and keyed the data into the computer correctly. It worked according to the design specifications of my programming. I was proud to see it work the way I designed it to work. The flawed output was no better than the input that resulted in failure. The first three times I attempted to get the proper results, they were flawed because the input was flawed. When I corrected the input, I received good output. I heard someone say, "Stop using failure habits in an attempt to get successful results." The machine worked properly when I stopped using flawed data to acquire successful results.

Information from your environment forms your thoughts, which ultimately contribute to an attitude of poverty or an attitude of prosperity. An attitude of poverty creates a condition of economic distress and dependence on others. An attitude of prosperity creates a condition of independence and prosperous living. You are your personal programmer, and now is your chance to correct your programming and to believe that you can produce better results in your life. It worked for me!

Positive Attitude: An Accumulation of Thoughts

Your positive attitude is of utmost importance when you are working with people. Your attitude shows your degree of willingness to work with others to try and to find common interests to assist you if needed. People with a positive attitude seek to work with others because they are interested in others. When people have a positive attitude, they are more inclined to say "yes" when new adventures come their way. With a positive attitude, they will tend to say "yes" to an informed risk or they will more likely be willing to use faith when testing new ground.

Have you seen people in the office or in school whom everybody likes? They always have a smile on their face. They always have encouraging words. They believe in what's possible and expect good things to happen. When the boss calls them to the office, or when they receive long awaited letters from employment opportunities, they expect the best to happen.

My grandmother taught me to have a positive attitude toward people. She said, "Respect will take you where money will not." It was that small accumulation of positive thoughts that my family embedded in us kids that made a difference in the way we respect people today.

An older friend, whom I respected, helped to reveal my career. He encouraged me to use my drawing skills by enrolling at Denmark Technical College to learn engineering graphics and design technology. I want, so badly, to earn an education! I had a barrier, yet I maintained a positive attitude. My classes started at 8:00 a.m. and ended at 3:00 p.m. At 3:30 p.m., my eight-hours of employment started. For two years, I worked this shift, attended Denmark Technical College to earn an Associate Degree.

After graduating from Denmark Technical College, my attitude about my ability changed. I developed a bigger dream. I had to work smarter and harder and the condition of my thoughts had to change and to grow, also. My thoughts had to be upgraded to achieve new possibilities. In this case, I wanted to improve my education in order to achieve my new dream of becoming an engineer. Therefore, for the next four years, I was an employee at South Carolina State University and as well as a student there pursuing a Bachelor of Science degree in Mechanical Engineering Technology. Because my mother instilled in me a vision to earn a higher educational degree, I followed that vision through to its final conclusion. She saw it as a means of self-help and independent living. My mother's foresight and vision began paying off in my senior year at South Carolina State University, because I landed several engineering offers from across the nation.

Correct Thinking — Desirable Circumstances

Thinking can cause desirable circumstances; however, thinking can also cause undesirable circumstances to occur. I will not address the thinking that's involved in producing undesirable circumstances to occur in a person's life. Instead, I will discuss the insight into the cause and effect relationship, which grew out of a person's thinking and which resulted in desirable circumstances.

I know of a family who is living a debt-free life-style; they are multimillionaire in the Amway business. They can pay cash for any type of car, home or almost any private airplane, including employing a pilot. They are a happy family, very involved in the community. They own real estate and business enterprises. When most people see them, they say they are lucky. However, they missed it by a mile. The real truth is that their success came because of positive thinking, working smart and helping a lot of people achieve their dreams before they acquired their wealth and life-style.

The life-style I just described did not *cause* their wealth. Their life-style is the *effect* of their dreams. The true *cause* was the dream they had that preceded the life-style and the work and effort which flowed from it. When success occurs, the *effect* is always glamorous to most people because they like the trappings of this level of achievement. Most people are not willing to invest the time and effort and to risk their money to pay the price to acquire the life-style. Some people believe that they can hold on to their old attitude of gratifying their bodies by drinking, partying, recreating activities and keeping their old habits and fears without sacrificing anything, and somehow achieve their dreams. P*sycho-cultivation* teaches that you have to change your thought pictures to move on to a higher level of achievement.

How do people arrive at the station in life where they are financially secure? They arrive at this station in life because of correct thinking and their desire, abiding faith, tenacious effort, dream, and commitment to serve hundreds or thousands of people. The *cause* was inspired by their dream that made them decide to change their attitude about success. This change in attitude creates a state of mind that says, I claim and believe the existence of this dream and it is already mine; I claim and believe it and I will do what it takes to make it a reality!

The *cause* is the situation or the dream that originated the action, which created the circumstances. The *cause* is the initial purpose for doing something. Before a dream is fulfilled, the *effect* was there in the form of a dream. The dream was the invisible pulling desire that caused the *effect* to be manifested.

When you look at your circumstances, you are seeing the effects of your past thoughts. Your thought pictures cause the current good or bad circumstances of your life. The good news is that you can change your life when you change your thought pictures. Changing lives requires changing your input. By reading self-development books, and seeking out self-enhancing people, you can accomplish goals. The bad news is that you have to be willing to leave your comfort zone in order to change.

CHAPTER 8

Conflict Resolution, Intervention, and Prevention

Controlling Crises in Life

Conflict resolution" is based on the idea that everyone can find a nonviolent solution to a potential conflict if he or she is willing. If this idea were not true, then humans would not be equipped with communicative and reasoning skills for determining effective approaches to problems. If we did not have these aforementioned skills, our solution to conflicts would take place at the survival level, as it does with animals. Instead of using our body limbs and parts for constructive purposes, they would be used for destructive purposes—fighting, killing etc. All of our intellectual attributes, as well as physical attributes, would seem to imply that someone of superior intellect had a purpose for human construction.

The Creator's intent is for humans to have a purpose to serve others. Because we have a purpose to serve others, our service should include what is positive and beneficial to humans. When two or more people come together, a relationship is formed. It does not matter whether the relationship is acknowledged or not, it does exist. If we have honor and respect as our goal, a harmonious relationship with another will overshadow any differences. I believe that people can evolve to the point where they can find solutions for effective conflict resolution, crime prevention, drug abuse, crime, poverty, violence and depraved human conditions.

Once you realize and understand that each of us is on a path leading to some destination or purpose, you will naturally want to help others reach their destination. Any conflict, that occurs, happens because we have lost focus of the beneficial nature of serving.

Everyone can learn from the life of a server. When a person becomes disgruntled or commits crimes, the person has started on another path, the path of a taker. Being a taker has, in many instances, caused the loss of a life in a relationship which has gone wrong.

There are four ideas for resolving a potential conflict that I will be covering. I have mentioned the topic serving the relationship which will be dealt with further. The other topics are forecast thinking, blowing out the fires of conflict and psychosocial modeling.

Serving the Relationship

In every conflict the disputants try to advance their position. The opportunity to come to a meeting of the minds can occur when we serve the relationship that exists between the two. When the relationship is served, the outcome produces a "win-win" solution. When two or more people are gathered together in peace or in conflict, a relationship is formed at that moment.

In this era of music and television popularity, our children are greatly influenced by the early overexposure to sex and violence. Inappropriate entertainment interferes with the parent-child relationship by competing with the parents' value system. Psychosocial modeling is a useful strategy in countering and responding to undesired values. When psychosocial modeling is used, it teaches a youngster a value system and it predisposes the youngster to options—the options and virtues taught will be no better than his or her teacher. Parents should take an interest in the relationships their children form with other children. Because from those relationships, a consensus will be made as to what activities they will be involved in. Since they are peers, the members of this relationship will be subjected to strong peer pressure to assimilate. As parents, we hope in the case of wrong doing our youngsters or teenagers will disassociate themselves from the group and not participate.

If we assemble for the purpose of peace, our bonds are

strengthened. Conversely, when we come together in conflict, our bonds are weakened. However, the relationship still exists. In both cases, when the best interest of the relationship is served, everyone goes away with his or her ego intact. Serving is just an attribute of love. If you love someone, you will not steal from or kill him or her. The relationship is the key to love for without it you would have no one to be the subject of the emotion of love. When you teach people how to model correct behavior, resolve conflicts by moving from the physical and emotional state of mind to thinking logically, they begin to serve the relationship.

The psychosocial model technique helps to develop options and encourages you to consider the consequences of your choices. Being a follower and carrying out the vision of a criminal has some undesirable consequences such as disappointed family members, crime victims, incarceration, loss of dignity, pain or death.

Learning to negotiate situations more effectively is an important skill in life. There are many ways to handle a conflict. However, being pre-exposed to proper conflict resolution tools are what today's youths need in their bag of life-skills. Another way of viewing how to handle conflicts can be described in the relationship between the salesman and customer. Customers have no training to prepare themselves against such skilled salesmen, yet customers have the greatest power. They have power to say "no" to the salesperson, if the product or service does not meet their needs. Salespeople don't want "No," as a response, so they learn techniques to handle their customers' objections. Sales managers coach their sales people on how to handle a customers' potential "No" which is an inherent impediment in the sales process. It takes someone who has superior skills to teach someone else how to have a better relationship, handle rejections, resolve conflicts, etc.

The "gang-bangers" or bullies become hot heads when they are fighting other gangs over turf boundaries. They try to sell each other on fighting. They are like high pressure salesmen who try to get you to buy their product or service. The hot heads know all of the techniques to provoke a fight. The high pressure salesperson knows how to apply pressure on the customers. The "gang-bangers" know how to provoke you with profanity, to talk about your mother, to threaten you, and to even destroy your property. They become emotionally upset at times when the average person would be calm. Society has ways of handling them. Yet, society does not get involved unless there is a crime. Therefore, when you are confronted with hot heads, you must learn how to cool them down. They want to be appreciated and respected so give them what they want. You must realize that your role in any matter is simply to remain calm. You have the power; you don't have to buy what they have to sell—violence. You can say "No" to violence. Find a way!

CHARACTER BENCHMARK: LESSON # 4

Conflict Resolution Ideas

The following are some ideas you can try:
1. If people level verbal attacks at you, listen to see if you might have done something to them without knowing. If so, apologize to them, and work to win them over to your way of thinking.
2. If you did do something to offend them, and if you can identify with their position, try to win them over by pointing out your oversight. It's important that you let them know that you do not intend to solve this dispute by fighting.
3. As stated above, if you have had a disagreement with others, your obligation is to maintain a dialogue, if at all possible. Let others know that you do not wish to have a conflict, but that you would rather work the situation out. If you can safely walk away, do so.
4. Only engage in a physical altercation, if it is necessary to pre serve your life. If you have done what you can to avoid an altercation, then it's in the hands of nature—"the first law of nature is self-preservation."

Forecast Thinking

I was watching television one evening and the weather man was forecasting the weather. He stated that there was going to be a fifty percent chance of rain on tomorrow. What he was essentially saying was that you had better be prepared because there was a real good chance it would rain. Therefore, I went out the next day prepared for the rain. It happened to have rained that day just as it was forecasted.

Forecast thinking works on prediction, which is about the same as what is done with the weather. Forecast thinking is having the ability to anticipate the actions of people with positive or negative character propensity and what they would do in a given situation. The accent is placed on a person's propensity for doing good or evil. Once the character disposition is decided, then based on your principles, you can decide to associate or disassociate with that person.

In a sense, it is utilizing the wisdom of discernment. It's being able to reason ideas out by listening to people to determine whether their plans are benevolent or malevolent. It is visualizing consequences to determine whether your actions will lead to serving or helping people. It may only take one negatively imbedded thought picture to create activity which produces the attitude of a taker. A person with an attitude of a taker can be easily determined by his or her conversations, habits or actions. He or she will be the one to ask you to risk taking something or harming someone.

Being aware of your purpose as a server and not a taker, should keep you on a more productive path in life. If you have a one percent chance of abusing drugs, of getting pregnant as a teen, or of harming someone, don't do it. Forecast and think of the consequences, get help, and refuse to get off the path that leads to the fulfillment of your goals and dreams.

Some people believe that it is possible to do something enticing only once, yet knowing it is wrong, because their chances of getting caught are low. This is wrongful thinking. This thinking will cause them to cross the bridge and succumb to the attitude of a taker. By embracing those habits, there is a 100% chance of losing their innocence as servers. When people become takers, they walk a dangerous path which can lead to their getting hurt, locked up in prison or killed. However, no matter how bad people think they have become, they can change by forecasting positive thought pictures which will change their actions, character and destiny.

Blowing Out the Fires of Conflict

Conflict resolution attempts to solve a disagreement among people with opposing viewpoints in a mutually beneficial manner. History can tell the stories of fatal or futile attempts to solve a conflict without allowing the other person some dignity. At the heart of resolving a conflict are differences and disregard for the other person's viewpoint. Almost everyone is concerned with saving face, protecting the ego and ending up in a position of respect.

Men or women who deliver scriptural messages are respected for their leadership. Doctors and nurses are respected for their abilities to assist in the process of healing. People in organizations and businesses are respected for their service to the community. However, every month litigation is brought against these public servants because people may have felt that they were wronged by them. When these public servants want to resolve a conflict, they don't fight as a method of solving conflicts. When a solution is needed, they usually resolve it through mediation or litigation. These individuals manage to keep the conflict at the talking stage. Some individuals allow their conflict to degrade into a physical conflict. Therefore, first step in correcting a conflict is to get the parties to respect each other's right to an opinion, even if they don't agree. Everyone is entitled to an opinion.

I was driving with my family one evening when a discussion came up with my wife, Marcia, concerning a conflict between two parties she was observing several years ago. She settled the conflict. At the end of the story she said, "I had to blow out their fire." What she meant was that she calmed them down in order to get the parties to think clearly and to talk. A cool head is what is needed to be safe during a conflict. One of the disputants has to be willing to blow out the fire so there can be a meeting of the minds.

The following are eight steps for blowing out the fires of conflict, in order to solve problems:

CHARACTER BENCHMARK: LESSON # 5

Blowing Out The Fires of Conflict

1. Both parties should *acknowledge* the *other's right* to having differing view points.
2. Each party needs to *voice* his or her *position* in a non-accusatory way and free from interruptions.

3. Each party should *write or voice* one moderate *solution.*
4. Each party should *assume the other's position* to identify with his or her point of view.
5. Each party should *reverse roles to their original positions.*
6. Each party should *compare* his or her *remedy* for an equitable outcome in behalf of the other party.
7. Each party should *agree to compromise* to gain a position that is harmonious and a win-win scenario for both parties.

One of the main values parents try to cultivate in their children is a sense of respect for them as their caregivers. I can appreciate parents' wanting to instill this value. We want our children to learn to become productive citizens. To be happy, to be disciplined and to be ethical, require that our children learn to respect education, employment, and other people.

Often, parents fall into the trap of trying to appease their children. They end up compromising the very virtues they are trying to instill. Remember, if you are teaching the youth the correct way to take on the responsibilities of life, you should not teach them to gravitate toward the convenient or expedient paths in life. Children are looking for boundaries, love, respect, your time, and a sense of well-being. If you allow children to rear themselves, you dilute your value system and cause them to disrespect you and what you are trying to teach them.

Intervention for Drugs and Violence

Psychosocial modeling involves mentally acting out or role-playing social dramas that occur in life. When people decide to take action in a conflict physically against another, they are often doing so from an emotional state of mind. They interpret events as being disrespectful or a violation of their rights which cause them to chose an option such as fighting. The goal of psychosocial modeling is to attempt to get people to act out these life dramas before such conflicts prevail. When we are able to get people to act out their conflicts in this type of setting, they are being given a pre-solution option, a more effective way of handling conflicts.

In psychosocial modeling, "what if" questions are ask by the facilitator. Facilitators with appropriate strategies can help improve youths' coping skills. The youth can be made to act out psychosocial dramas through role playing. These activities will prepare youths to make better choices. The key is to prevent individuals from undertaking negative activities.

CHARACTER BENCHMARK: LESSON # 6

Role Playing Activities

Sometimes the person introducing you to illegal drugs will not be a drug dealer. The preceding activities are conflict resolution and psychosocial role playing scenarios. Consider each situation by circling "yes" or "no" under each of the two headings (drug dealer or friend) as to whether you will perform the activities **one** though **eleven** with a drug dealer or a friend. Next, write the reason why you have chosen each answer. Then, discuss each of your conclusions or share your insights with a youth supporter or parent(s). A drug dealer or your friend may approach you to do the following illegal activities - choose your answers carefully:

Activities	Drug dealer	Friend
1. to sell drugs (ex. marijuana)	yes or no	yes or no

Why ____

____

____

2. to join the gang	yes or no	yes or no

Why ____

____

____

3. to drop drugs off	yes or no	yes or no

Why ____

____

____

4. to ride with him	yes or no	yes or no

Why ____

____

____

Activities	**Drug dealer**	**Friend**
5. to just hang out	yes or no	yes or no

Why ____
____
____

6. to hurt someone	yes or no	yes or no

Why ____
____
____

7. to steal	yes or no	yes or no

Why ____
____
____

8. to use drugs (ex. marijuana)	yes or no	yes or no

Why ____
____
____

9. to kill someone	yes or no	yes or no

Why ____
____
____

10. to quit school	yes or no	yes or no

Why ____
____
____
____

11. to disobey your parents	yes or no	yes or no

Why ____
____
____

PART 5

Attitude for Success # 4:

Transforming Adversity into Building Blocks for Success

Adversity

The fourth stage, the Adversity Stage, occurs as the plant is placed in its environment. This is where the plant begins to obey its call to become a giver and to be fruitful and multiply. The outcome, which is what the plant is supposed to look like and to produce, has already been programmed into the plant's genetic makeup.

In the case of a tomato plant, in order to become successful and to live out its purpose to serve, a number of conditions must be met. All of these conditions amount to a plant being in a particular environment. The plant has to exist in this environment or it will live its life out of character—nonproductive.

After the seed of a plant has been placed in its environment of success, it grows. The roots of the plant begin to force itself down as the plant grows upward. The physical world that surrounds it begins to challenge its destiny. The earth does not soften to its growth, and the rocks and adversities don't volunteer to move out of its path. True to its purpose, the plant continues to obey the genetic messages locked up in its cell body. So, it breaks through this tremendous barrier which is the surface layer of earth, that contained it.

Once the tomato plant has broken through the earth, harsh elements of nature await to challenge its resolve. The weeds also enter the picture and begin to fulfill their destiny as a taker. The weeds begin to compete with the plant for the nutrients in the soil. The weed associates itself closely with the plant with the intent to take from it the nutrients of life. The weed is not mobile like other pests that prey on the plant. No, the weed coexists nearby, competing for water, sunlight, and nutrients by draining and sucking slowly the life potential and the plant's possibility of becoming productive. The weed's nature is that of a taker, it takes from the life of the plant.

Like the tomato plant, despite what your environment is, you have to accept what it is and press forward toward your dreams. To realize the state of mind experienced by a winner, people must place themselves into their *success environment. Certain psychological conditions have to be right for a person to grow and change.*

People must maintain a positive attitude, believe in themselves and have a dream which compels them forward. If difficulties happen in their lives to cause things to be less than ideal, then they must be willing to make personal changes and become masters over their environment.

CHAPTER 9

Converting Adversity Into Success

The Environment of Success

According to an old African proverb, "Struggle makes one strong." Adversities are part of success. Anyone who claims to have achieved any measure of success will credit adversities as being, at first a pest, but later a necessary impediment that caused her or his inborn attributes to surface. Self-confidence, leadership, faith, hope, and intense desire are all forged through adversity. The ideal outcome of adversity is to develop into one who can overcome and achieve dreams.

The real you, the spiritual part of your makeup, is not limited to the physical realm. When seemingly insurmountable adversities appear in your life, it is important for you to get help spiritually through prayer. Take action as if what you are seeking will occur. Faith cultivates "a can-do attitude," which creates positive thought pictures to fuel your quest to overcome your circumstances. With faith, you can come to see that adversities are small building blocks of success.

You don't have to live with a feeling of hopelessness when you are confronted with difficulty; you can decide to overcome them. Stop and let the principles on *psycho-cultivation* show you how. You will be inspired to get up and realize that overcoming adversity is a prelude to success.

Transforming the Struggles of Adversities into Success

Struggling with adversity and finally defeating it are experiences which are part of your success. You will find the struggle to be painful and success pleasurable. While accessing an upcoming event as being unpleasant, success comes when you are willing to undertake the process. The choices that you make when confronted with adversity may often attract new circumstances associated with that decision.

You should continue to seek your dreams despite adversities and to go on and to win. The struggle will begin to lose its hold on you when you get closer to the reward. When the pain from struggling is gone, the emotional string that held you in the past begins to unravel. To move forward, if problems block your progress, you are probably focusing on adversities and not focusing on your dreams. When a salesperson sits and glares at the telephone before making calls to customers, the salesperson experiences unsettling feelings due to the struggle within. The salesperson does not want to experience the emotion that is associated with the outcome, if someone says "No." The solution lies in correcting the conflict between willpower and the imagination. If the salesperson gives up, then the struggle has ended and a failed attempt has been recorded in the mind. By not attempting to call, in affect, the salesperson still gets the "no" he so badly wanted to avoid.

When a struggle starts and a barrier is confronted, the outcome may be negative or positive. Yet, the outcome should be respected because it becomes your teacher and you are its student. When I was growing up, I did not realize that my humble beginnings in the rural section of town made it obvious that my family was not wealthy. Sure, the conditions were not to our liking, but our mother had us focusing on a vision, a vision that elevated our thinking. Part of her vision was for her children to earn an education so that we could acquire the desires of our hearts. At every occasion, my mom reinforced her vision about our getting a higher education. My mom was able to see her vision come true because seven out of eight children finished high school. Four children finished college.

When I was growing up, many mornings I would hear my

mother say, "All right kids, its time to get up and get ready for school." My four sisters, three brothers, two cousins and I would all start getting ready for school. We would walk a short distance in front of the old house to catch the bus. When I came home from school, sometimes I had to help lead my great-grandmother around because she was blind. As I look back, there were difficulties in our household, but the grown-ups' example taught us how to handle them successfully.

I liked seeing my granddaddy plow the fields with the mules. He would say words and make sounds to the mules and they did what he wanted them to do. In my home environment, I saw excellence. My family worked hard in the face of life's struggles, and I find the lessons of those experiences continually floating to the surface of my thinking.

My life-style seems like a tale out of the old world. I believe my humble rural living was good for me because it isolated me from some of the entrapments of youth. Many youths from the city were exposed to cigarettes and drinking early in life. I began to be exposed to some of these youthful entrapments later in life after my values and principles were established. I had many temptations when I was growing up in the 60s, but my principles guided my decisions.

One of my most vivid work experiences occurred when my granddaddy took my brothers, cousin and me into the corn fields to harvest corn. The owner's harvester gathered the corn and granddaddy was given the freedom to enter the property and glean what was left. To the untrained eye, the field was worthless before we entered. Granddaddy Linzy Islar saw the field as an opportunity to earn money, and he was able to reap a tidy sum of money from selling the corn that was left in the field.

Granddaddy would have us help him load the wagon with corn. I would climb right up there with him on the weather-worn seat at the front of the wagon. Granddaddy would make a clicking sound or two and give a light yank on the leather straps which was attached to bits located in the mule's mouth. Upon hearing the clicking sounds and feeling the yank of the straps, the mules would start to move. The leather straps were attached to a bit inside the mouth of the mule. The ride was rough, because the surface of the wheels consisted of a thin band of metal fasten to a wooden frame. I could feel almost every rock while riding on the wagon. Granddaddy positioned the mule out of the path of our work. After we had piled several stacks, granddaddy would drive the mule to the first stack and so on. We children did the loading as well as much of the picking. When we finished loading the wagon to capacity, we rode in the wagon to the market and sold the corn.

Mom worked hard, and her earnings were meager. Often we were playing or doing chores when we would see Mom coming home with a plate of food in her hands. This was a routine for her; she was allowed to bring home food from her work as a maid. We all knew that it would be feasting time in a little while. The food mom brought home supplemented the meal Grandma Ethel Islar cooked.

The only one who did not get to eat at the dinner table every day was my stepfather James Willis, Sr. He worked as a brakeman for a railroad company in Florida, nearly two hundred and fifty miles away from our home in Denmark, South Carolina. James would come home only on the weekends.

Sometimes, if you want the fruits of success, you might have to go where it is or do what possessing it demands. You may have to see the opportunity in the wasteland which everyone has passed by and turned the wasteland into a profitable venture. If you look for success past the adversities, you will find it!

The Power of Rebuke

Psycho-cultivation is similar to a management system which will alert you to negative thought pictures so they can be effectively dealt with. *Psycho-cultivation* works because it becomes the process manager of a person's life and it refuses to allow the negative thought pictures to "go to work." If you are positive, negative thought pictures will cause doubt. Practice thinking positively so that negative thinking will be diminished, thereby causing it to become weakened and atrophied through nonuse.

Many people have asked me, "How were you able to withstand the environment of prison and yet remain positive?" Though I did not understand it at the time, I used the "power of rebuke." I would in the name of Jesus Christ rebuke any doubt or negative thinking. The negative thoughts were rebuked and that helped me to maintain a hopeful and positive attitude by saying "No" to gloomy thoughts. My abiding faith in God was magnified. By praising God and giving Him Lordship over my problems, I was in a constant state of belief and faith in my deliverance. There were always moments in a 24-hour day to become negative about prison and about the injustice of it all. However, when a negative thought did enter my mind, I would use the power of rebuke, saying, "Satan, I rebuke you in the name of Jesus Christ! I claimed the belief that would God free me and clear my name and any other thoughts to the contrary were from Satan!"

When I was alone, depressed and in the darkness of the prison, the Word of God served me. The scriptures served and comforted me by helping to amplify my belief through their promises that those who believe will be vindicated and freed.

I did not know what timetable God was using before He would open the bars and free me. However, I did know that when it was time for Him to free me, no steel bars, no concrete and not even the total gravitational pull of all the masses in the universe would be strong enough to hold me there!

Like the seed, we humans come into the world with a pre-programmed purpose to serve. Serving is the constant in a person's preprogramming. The manner in which we discharge our service defines how constructive and useful our actions are to God, to our country and to each other. Everything we do serves either a good or a bad purpose. We have the option of providing employment, or providing illegal drugs; earning an education or dropping out of school. All are examples of the duality of human nature and of serving a benevolent or malevolent purpose. In the underworld of crime, serving a malevolent cause is prevalent. Criminals produce goods and services for selfish reasons and for the reckless personal needs of others.

We are packaged with intelligence to reshape matter and improve on life in accordance with our desired purpose to serve. A builder reshapes matter; for example, trees are used, and arranged into a beautiful place for us to live in or reshaped into beautiful furniture to sit on. You can reshape your thought pictures by rebuking negative thought pictures at the moment of occurrence so they can be reshaped into dream thoughts using the principles of *psycho-cultivation*.

Having a Motto of Life

An effective technique for attacking difficulties is to have powerful mottoes. A motto is a personal rule that is adopted to live by. These personal rules are usually not abandoned. If mottoes are honored, they become strong anchors. When adversities mount up, I borrow one of my wife's conquering mottoes, "Nothing can impede my progress!" In other words, maintain until you obtain. When I use this powerful statement, I don't worry about the adversities, because my state of mind becomes focused on my dreams. I am elevated in mind to a more productive and positive mode.

"When the going gets tough, the tough get going," I heard someone say. I agree with this motto because it gives me strength to endure. Sometimes adversities can eat your positive attitude for lunch, figuratively speaking. A motto is just another way to get you into a more productive state. At times, when the going got really tough, I found comfort in using Paul's scriptural words as one of my mottoes of life, "I can do all things through Christ who strengthens me," Philippians 4:13. I didn't say it just once. I said it hundreds of times until my subconscious mind convinced my belief system that with Christ all things are possible!

CHARACTER BENCHMARK: LESSON # 7

Ten Myths Associated With Overcoming Adversity

Myth No. 1:
There is but so much opportunity out there.

There is really no such reality as a lack of opportunity, if you have a dream. Lack of opportunity occurs because your focus is on someone else's dream or personal problems. You are trying to enlist yourself in someone else's dream. The solution is to step out on faith and create your own opportunity or possibilities.

Myth No. 2:
There is no use trying, they won't let me go but so far.

This type of thinking is called the glass ceiling syndrome. It is the contention that other people can limit your achievements in life. Your attitude will become an "it is no use trying" type of attitude which translates into a feeling that there is no hope, or there is a feeling of resignation. Doing indicates to your mind that you have a goal that will not be denied by experiences with adversities. You should not allow your success to be dependent solely on others; if so, they can, at will, deny you that success.

Myth No. 3:
I tried and nothing happened; I might as well quit.

A person who quits has developed a habit of quitting. You don't have any staying power. Use affirmations and work on your belief and confidence. You can never win, if quitting is an option. You must believe that what you desire will be realized. If you do not succeed at first, second, third and so forth and so on try, try again.

Myth No. 4:
They are holding me back.

No one can really hold you back in life without first holding themselves back. This attitude is similar to Myth No. 2. You have the ability, but you have experienced a few setbacks or roadblocks. It may seem to you that other people may be preventing you from progressing further. Check, introspectively, to see if you may have legitimate personal problems which may require that you change some things in your life. If there are no personal problems, try another avenue up the corporate ladder. If this doesn't work, take your unappreciated knowledge and skills and move on and help someone else become more profitable using your vast experience.

If someone tries to hold you back, they are contributing lots of physical and mental energy, money or effort to hold you back. Use that energy and slingshot yourself into another door of possibilities and create your opportunity. The person holding you back cannot effectively do it and progress at the same time.

Myth No. 5:
I don't want to be odd—my peers may disassociate me.

Peer pressures are influences from people in your age group and from your environment. If you succumb, you put your own better judgment in neutral, while you trust your peer's opinion. For this reason, parents should instill virtues in children when they are young. If your virtues are not solidly rooted, your child will be hard pressed to end up an independent thinker. If the foundation is strong, the child will be strong. A youth needs to know that it is OK to say "No" when something is not in his or her best interest.

Myth No. 6:
Trying illegal drugs won't lead to drug abuse.

Taking illegal drugs is a sign that you have much more to learn about yourself. You feel that you are not equipped to bring pleasure into your life. Since you feel that you can't bring the peace of mind or the pleasurable state of mind naturally, you turn to drugs. When you delegate control of your life to drugs, you will do some weird things. Some drug abusers have killed, stolen, lied, and hurt family members and others for drugs. The solution is to eliminate illegal drugs as an option and to broaden the list of things that bring adventurous experiences and spiritual growth to your life. Drug abusers get pleasure as they serve themselves, yet the greatest sense of service and pleasure comes from helping others.

Myth No. 7:
Racism means that other people are better than me.

Racism happens when people are attempting or controlling a person's destiny because they have a false belief that their race is superior. Racist people focus on the differences among people in an attempt to show how they are better. They believe that the color of their skin, their socioeconomic status, and their heritage make them better than other people. This false superiority complex is a cover for a deep-seated inferiority complex and a weakness they are trying to hide.

A normal, healthy, non-racist person will believe that all people are created equal. Normal people will focus on what brings us together and how we are similar. They will believe that all people are capable, and that it's up to them to express it. The color of one's skin does not denote superiority, nor does it suggest inferiority.

Only your service, moral standing and productive make you a superior server among the diversity of ethnic groups. There is no superior race of people. A healthy mentality realizes that other people aren't inferior because God didn't make any mistakes when He created people. God created man and woman in his spiritual image and no human being is inferior to another!

Myth No. 8:
I'm a teenager but I want a child; my friends have babies.

One thing that ruins the lives of teenagers is parenting a child before completing their education and getting married. They see an infant and fall in love with the little one. They do not realize the awesome responsibility that goes with rearing a child. An infant's needs are tremendous; therefore, a person must be mature enough to meet these needs.

There is also the moral side. Is it right to parent a child outside of marriage? Granted, children are born to unmarried mothers every day. There are many successful single parent families but involvement by both parents, in a two parent household, is best for the child. There were many occasions and many experiences I missed because my biological father was not there to meet my needs.

Parenting a child when one is not even old enough to sign a binding contract is not recommended. The best time to start having children is when you are mature, independent, working and married.

Myth No. 9:
I feel inferior around certain people; I'm not good enough.

An inferiority complex occurs when you think you don't measure up to others. Again, this is a way of trying to conform to others, which works against the concept of being an independent thinker. You have to believe in yourself and your abilities by knowing that no one is created greater than you. Additionally, you have to reach back into the ancestry of your people and find some heroes. If even one person from your ancestry succeeded, then you can do great things, too.

Myth No. 10:
I don't believe that I can do it.

Self-doubt and lack of confidence is having little faith in your own ability to perform. Individuals cannot achieve their goals, if they doubt that they can bring it into reality. It is a good idea to think good things about yourself. Powerful mottoes can help to strengthen weak areas of your life. For example, if you are a student make an affirmation; such as, "If it is in a book I can learn it." Or if you work for a company say, "I am a good employee and am producing the best quality product that can be produced."

The key here is to get working on the inside—the self-image. Once the fractured self-image is well adjusted again, you can begin to operate from an empowered position in life. You will believe that you have what it takes. When the self-image of an individual is not strong, the individual often uses the phrases, "I don't believe," or "I can't do." When the self-image of a person is strong, he or she will make statements as follows: "I believe I can," or "I can do it."

Expecting to Overcome Adversities in all Sports

In sports, a player doesn't give-up if he or she is stopped while running a play. In life, when confronted with difficulties, you should not give up. However, sometimes former players, as well as others, forget these lessons and give up. If the team fails to move the ball forward, the team does not quit. Do you quit when your plans move at a snail's pace or show no indication of succeeding?

If players have to play in rain or snow, they keep playing, unless the game is called off. When the path gets dirty and muddy, do you stay with your values and keep going until you fulfill your purpose and dreams? In life, the game is to achieve enough little goals to make the dream come true.

In the game of football, the object of the game is to make the most field goals and touchdowns to win the game. In football, the players' attitudes are adjusted to expect adversities to occur and their attitudes are maintained to overcome them. Talent, techniques, and attitude invariably contribute to the successful outcome of a winning team. Adversities are expected in every game and teams have an offensive coach and a defensive coach to plan with that in mind.

In the tryouts, the coaches weed out the marginal players so that the most talented players are left—the cream of the crop. In high school or college, a player may have played a specific position. However, in professional football, his talents will be reassessed and he will be placed in a position to best utilize his talents to the fullest. Once you make the team, you have to continue to use your talents to the best of your ability, so that you remain on the team.

Next, new players are reprogrammed into the mind-set of the team. The coaches, then, teach them new techniques. These elite players are taught the communication system of the team, called plays. The plays are of the utmost importance because while on the field, players have only a few moments to grasp the quarterback's intentions. The plan is to get the team moving as a unified force toward its goal. If everyone carries out his part in spite of expected barriers, the play is designed to create a touchdown. I might add, just about every play is designed to convert into a touchdown or field goal. A team which is unprepared will find itself the loser at the end of the game.

Finally, one of the most important parts of a player's conditioning is his attitude. Coaches want their players to be motivated for success. They want players to know that winning is a must, not an option. The coach motivates the players by telling them how good winning is and how its going to be as the new champs. He tells them how good they are, that they are the best, that he believes in them, and that they can do it.

In order to make it happen big in your life, you need a personal attitude coach, similar to a football coach. However, you will act as your own personal attitude coach and be self-motivated through positive affirmations, encouraging thought pictures, praise, and focus of thoughts on your dream. Your personal attitude coach is interested in you making the winning team so that you can succeed and achieve your dreams.

CHARACTER BENCHMARK: LESSON # 8

Overcoming Adversity to Win the Game of the Century

When you study sports, you realize that to win in sports, you have to struggle and overcome the built in obstacles of the game before you win. The game of the century could actually be you versus your current problems. Will you win? When you possess the attitude that you write the script for your success and you never give up, you will win!

This story illustrates the need to look at adversities in a different way. When you understand the concept of how to negotiate adversity, you will become empowered and resourceful enough to overcome adversity.

We will begin our hypothetical story in the last quarter. The announcer says, "The game is in the last few minutes of the quarter between the biggest rival football teams in the conference." This is a dynamic game between the Positive Producers team and Negative Non-producers team. It's the game of the century! Everybody has sided with his or her team and the stakes are high.

Over the past three years the Producers have been the conference winners. This year the Non-producers have recruited a real talent, No. 85—Self Doubt. The coach of the Non-producers is hoping that Self Doubt can work his magic on the Positive Producers' self confidence. There are 100,000 people watching the game live in the largest stadium in the world.

The announcer introduces the challengers, the Non-producers team, and the stadium is filled with "boos" and "yeas." The following Non-producer's members are introduced while they run toward their sideline: No. 50—"Lack of Opportunity," No. 88—"No Use Trying," No 24—"Quitter," No. 81—"They are Holding Me Back," No. 12—"Peer Pressure," No. 19—"Drug Abuser," No. 53—"Racism," No. 62—"Teen Pregnancy," No. 20—"Inferiority Complex," No. 99—"Crime" and No. 85—"Self Doubt." Folks, now you have it! The challengers from the little town of Takersville, United States.

"Ladies and gentlemen, I want to present to you, your champions, the Producers'!" The crowd turns into a roaring noise box, with piercing thunder of claps, yells, cheers, and team chants. The announcer calls the names of the following Producers members as they run toward their sideline: No. 49, "Opportunity," No. 87—"Keep Trying," No. 23—"Never Quit," No. 82—"Nothing Holds Me Back," No. 11—"Peer Support," No. 18—"Drug Free," No. 52—"Equality," No 61—"Pregnancy Free Teen," No. 19— "Achiever," No. 84—"Confidence." Your champions, the Positive Producers, from the big city of Giversville, United States. The referee signals for the Non-Producers team to kick off to the Producers.

Begin by answering the game play questions one through six. At the end of the five game plays, maintain the same state of mind as a football player who does not regard taking adversities too seriously, but acknowledging them, and continuing until you win.

Sample game play: Instructions: Circle the best answer.

The Producers have the ball and they are stopped at the Non-producer's team 31 yard line. First down, the ball is snatched and No. 88—"Quitter" approaches. The ball is thrown to No. 84—"Confidence, " and No. 52—"Equality," blocks when he... The best game play is letter "c".

a. stops and quit.
b. gets tackled by No 68—"No Use Trying, " no gain.
c. spins and keep moving for 3 yard gain
d. drops to the ground.

Instructions: Complete the following game plays one through five by circling the best or most progressive answer.

The punt —The game is tied with three minutes left. No one can predict the outcome of this highly contested game. No. 50—"Lack of Opportunity," punts the football and No. 49—"Opportunity" fair catches the ball on the opponent's 42 yard line. The following options are available; choose a progressive strategy by circling the appropriate letter:

a. stop and quit
b. get tackled by No. 50—"Lack of Opportunity."
c. Fair catch the ball on the opponent's 42 yard line
d. Do nothing.

First down, the ball is thrown. No. 87—"Keep Trying" catches the football. The Producers are stopped by No. 88—"No Use Trying" at the opponent's 48 yard line. The following options are available; choose a progressive strategy by circling the appropriate letter:

a. stop and quit
b. spin and keep moving for a 10 yard gain

c. get tackled by No 88—"No Use Trying " no gain
d. drop to the ground.

Second down, the game has become heated, the ball is snapped and No. 99—"Crime" approaches. The quarterback throws the ball to No. 23—"Never Quit " and he catches the ball and is stopped at the 33-yard line. The following options are available; choose a progressive strategy by circling the appropriate letter:
a. do nothing
b. hit the ground before No. 24—"Quit" gets there
c. stop
d. side step No. 99—"Crime" for a gain of 15 yards

Third down, the game is riveting and full of excitement! The ball is snapped and No. 36—"They are Holding Me Back" is rushing strong. The quarterback hands off the ball to No. 11—"Peer Support" and No. 18—"Drug Free" blocks for a gain of 21 yards. No. 11—"Peer Support" is stopped at the 12 yard line by No. 19—"Drug Abuser." The following options are available; choose a progressive strategy by circling the appropriate letter:
a. stiff arm No. 11—"Peer Pressure" and gain 21 yards
b. quickly hit the mud
c. get tackled by No. 19, "Drug Abuser"
d. let others think for you.

First down with 39 seconds left in the game. The ball is on the Non-producer's 12 yard line. The score is 6 to 6. The Producers have possession of the ball. Four of the Non-Producers biggest players No. 85—"Self Doubt," No. 53—"Racism," No. 62—"Teen pregnancy" and No. 20—"Inferiority Complex" plan to stop their play and regain the ball. The ball is snapped and No. 19—"Achiever," the quarterback runs back and to the right and he throws a long pass in the end zone and No. 82—"Nothing Holds Me Back," catches the ball for the touchdown. No. 54—"Confidence" kicks the extra point—it is good! The timer now shows only three seconds to go in the ball game. The kickoff followed with No. 68—"No Use Trying" of the Non-producers signaling for a fair catch. The Non-producers have three seconds to work their magic. The ball is hiked, and the quarterback throws a desperate pass to No. 88—"No Use Trying" and the football is knocked down by Producer No. 23—"Never Quit" and the time runs out.

Wow!! What a ball game—The Producers have won the game! We now know who will have the bragging rights for the next year. And you know, No. 85—"Self Doubt" could not stand up to the task against the awesome talents of No. 84—"Confidence". The following options are left; select what you would do:

CHARACTER BENCHMARK: LESSON # 9

Adapting the "Attitude for Success" in Real Life Situations

After playing the above game, Overcome Adversity to Win the Game of the Century, your mind will still be in a winning mode and still solution oriented. Then commit to looking at your problems in a new light and go on to achieve your most optimal outcome. To cultivate a winning attitude, you need to think, "I'm in life to win over my circumstances!" This should be your state of mind because you will be seeing the adversity as just an experience to overcome.

When you play this game, maintaining a state of mind which is necessary to win in the game of football, especially when obstacles are coming at you from all directions. With this new attitude, get ready to tackle your personal problems and adapt their possible solutions. Become determined to work your real life problems through to their ideal and most logical conclusion. When you have problems in your life, go to a huddle with good advisers to develop a plan: to confront them, to block them, to move around them, to overcome them and to become a success in the real life game you are dealt.

Make the following activities real by introducing your personal problems. List below five of your personal problems, then, adjacent to each of the problems list the five ideal solutions to each of the problems. As you play this game, remember to have a positive attitude as you pursue your ideal outcome to your problems!

Problems or Adversities	*Ideal Solutions or Outcome*
1st ______________________	1st ______________________
2nd ______________________	2nd ______________________
3rd ______________________	3rd ______________________
4th ______________________	4th ______________________
5th ______________________	5th ______________________

In order to overcome problems and get your ideal outcomes, you must have an attitude of tenacity, resolve, and determination. The sole purpose for having you do this activity and to play the game above is to remind you to maintain success as a state of mind in which adversity must be acknowledged and dealt with in order to achieve your dreams (outcomes). If you need to deal with the adversities in your life, get someone who can coach you through them and who can instill in you the determination to one day face your problems with determination to achieve the ideal solutions and outcomes.

Overcoming Adversity

Focusing and advancing toward fixed goals despite problems are how you overcome adversity. You have to accept that adversity will almost always be a part of an individual's formula for success. What most people don't do is allow for its presence. If you expect to have success, then allow for adversity. It will almost certainly appear in your affairs; once it is subdued, you will begin to gain mastery over your life situations. I teach people to welcome anything that challenges their resolve. When a problem is welcomed, the next step is for the problem to be studied, mastered, and discarded. To achieve success, you will not automatically arrive without some setbacks along the way. After accomplishing a goal you should start another. A series of goals and rewards can be used to motivate and to remind you to keep focusing on the dream.

Moving forward in the face of adversities establishes your desire to achieve—to realize your dream. Adversities form a relationship with you and become a part of your success because they awaken you. Overcoming adversities has always been the formula for progress and success. Since the beginning of time, man has been confronted with many adversities in life. The cave man solved his challenge of cold weather by moving into a cave and later discovering fire.

Many of us have experienced the loss of a loved one, a financial crisis or some other barrier. The way we handle adversities will determine whether we will experience success or failure. Adversities will be your companion along the road to achieving your dreams. However, the way you respond to these adversities will determine whether you have developed the key attitude that will release success in your life. Once you have discovered the key hidden within the lessons of difficulty, you will have joined the ranks of overcomers. That key can be found in practicing the principles discussed in *psycho-cultivation*.

My desire for you is to develop an attitude toward adversities that whenever there is an obstacle, the next thought that comes to your mind is what can I learn from this experience so that I can turn it around and realize success in my life?

What are adversities? They are an unwanted stumbling block or challenge that is in the path of achieving your dreams and goals. In order to consistently overcome adversity after adversity, your attitude must change. If you worked as a restaurant employee all your life, but now you want to set a new dream to become a doctor, you must acquire the necessary knowledge and skills. You must first receive your bachelor of science degree before applying to medical school. Once you are accepted at a medical school, you will gain the skills, training, techniques and attitude that are needed to become a doctor. Because you were willing to commit to making changes in your education, the journey toward your dream is assured, if you don't quit. When you are improving yourself, your mind is in a growth mode. All that is necessary for you to do is to move forward with faith and mount a frontal push toward realizing your dream.

During my bout with struggles associated with the "Texas Nightmare," I learned to draw on spiritual victories. I went to the Bible and read the story of Joseph in Genesis and how he was unjustly incarcerated. I *claimed and believed* the fact that just as

God delivered Joseph in the Bible, He can do the same for me.

Through courage, dreams and strength, African slaves in America overcame the harsh and cruel conditions of slavery. Many slaves did not know whether they would personally make it to freedom, but they had the desire and dream that one day they would be free men and women. Some of them took the dream of freedom into their own hands and others were freed later under the "color of the law."

It is left up to us to have faith, courage and desire, to overcome adversity. By never quitting, you can be a partner of faith with those who have survived the struggle and overcome adversities to win in the end. Others had to overcome adversities, and when you learn of what they had to undergo, you begin to realize that your struggles are nothing close to what they had to bear. Learning from the lives of heroes, we can acquire strength and courage to help others.

You can probably attest to the fact that in life there seems to be an abundance of struggles. The victories are far and between, but no one can deny the lessons learned from the struggles. What's lacking is your resolve to take the lessons in which you have invested your irreversible time regarding these struggles and benefit from them.

The goal is to help you see your current struggles and experiences as your next step toward success. When you begin to see it that way, you will be encouraged to move on past the struggle. Also, when you succeed, you will be able to reach down and pull others up because they can be helped by your experiences.

Graduating from college is one of the most significant dreams I have ever accomplished. I remember the struggles, hard work and effort that went into this proud moment in my life. The graduation ceremony was for us, the graduates and parents. We were seated on the football stadium grounds surrounded by hundreds of proud parents and friends.

Though graduating from college was a momentous accomplishment for me, I encountered some adversities with this success. When I arrived on campus the first year, I attended classes in the day and worked at night. That year my grades suffered and I was on academic probation. It was personally embarrassing for me, but yet I never considered quitting as an option! I continued improving until I finally overcame my barrier by reaching a balance where I could succeed in school while working. I knew I was going to graduate because I was not a quitter. I continued my college education until I succeeded in graduating.

After graduating, my next dream was to become employed as an engineer working for a large firm. I realized that dream when I accepted a position as an engineer at E-Systems. This led me to another dream, getting married and starting a family. Now I have more dreams. As you can see, after realizing goals and dreams, it's time to pursue new ones. The following ten rules on how to overcome adversity helped me during my "Texas Nightmare:"

CHARACTER BENCHMARK: LESSON # 10

Lenell Geter's Ten Rules To Overcome Adversity

Rule #1:
Have Faith in God.

Faith allows you to believe that the decisions and directions you have chosen will help you realize your dreams. Faith puts you in the spiritual realm of possibilities where the things you desire are possible. God is the spiritual source of faith that your dreams will be manifested. Your action statement is: I will have faith in God!

Rule #2:
Believe in Yourself.

Have confidence and belief in yourself. Always remember that your values define who you really are. Next, believe that the adversity you're confronting can be overcome. Begin to search for others who have overcome similar adversities. Don't rush into hasty decisions that conflict with your belief and value system. Remember all of your positive past victories in order to reinforce your belief in self. Imagine positive thought pictures of yourself having already achieved the goal. Your action statement is: I will believe in myself!

Rule #3:
Understand the Circumstances and Do Your Homework.

When confronted with an adversity, begin to do your homework. Understand what may have caused the situation and look closely at the circumstances and do research, find possible solutions. Your action statement is: I will understand the circumstances and do my homework.

Rule #4:
Know Your Rights.

In order to resolve problems in your life, you need to understand your rights. Knowing your rights should insulate you from violating the rights of others. Other people's rights are as important as yours. Valuing others' rights protect your rights at the same time. Your action statement is: I will learn my rights!

Rule #5:
Seek Experienced Help to Develop Your Action Plan.

The best solution to a dilemma can often be resolved from someone who has experience with your particular challenge. This person can often be a guide to you. For example, in the Texas experience, I used attorneys to handle the legal aspects of my case. Your action statement is: I will seek experienced help to develop my action plan!

Rule #6:
Get started. Put forth effort.

Getting yourself into action is pivotal toward resolving the problem or barrier. Nothing has ever been accomplished unless someone got started and put forth an effort. Your action statement is: I will get started and put forth an effort now!

Rule #7:
Focus on Your Purpose.

Why am I doing this? This question is best answered when you consider whether your actions are congruent with your purpose, virtues and beliefs. Once you are clear as to your purpose, there will be no hesitation in meeting and overcoming adversity. Your action statement is: I will focus on my purpose!

Rule #8:
Stay the Course.

Sometimes the course may get rough, and the adversities numerous, but you must stay on course. Possibly, other pathways may result while pursuing your vision which may take you to other prosperous and new possibilities. Other attractive possibilities that flow as a result of your plans may cause you to want to stray off course, but don't. Your action statement is: I will stay on course!

Rule #9:
Think: "I Can Do It."

Thinking, "I can do it," should dominate your thoughts every time you think about your realistic goals and dreams. When you look in the mirror, say out loud, "I can do it!" Your belief in yourself will help you to overcome your adversities. "I can do it," is often the first sign that you will realize your goal. Your action statement is: I will believe that I can do it!

Rule #10:
Never Give up and Never Quit.

If you decide that giving up is not an option, you will realize success. Success will reward you after you overcome each barrier. Eliminate the word "quit" from your vocabulary every time you decide to pursue your dreams and goals. Your action statement is: I will never give up and never quit!

PART 6

Attitude for Success # 5:

Fulfilling Family or Individual Dreams Through Benevolent Productivity

Productivity

Now that the tomato plant has passed its major barriers—the ground, periods of drought, the elements of nature, birds and animals—the fifth stage, the productive stage, occurs. This happens when the plant has matured and is ready to produce. At this juncture, the plant shows signs that it is ready to bear fruit.

All of the other stages the plant went through contributed toward strengthening it to fulfill its destiny. It's as if the plant went through a great deal just to contribute its product to the world. It produces a fruit that is good to eat. The plant becomes a giver, a producer, or an unselfish contributor.

When you focus on pursuing your dreams, you are wanting to become productive so you can fulfill your dream. Fulfillment comes after you have accomplished your dreams. Your life will cross all the adversities and traps out there, but never give-up on your dream. Become a producer, join the process and have a dream in which you can grow up to believe.

CHAPTER 10

Families or Individuals Succeeding Despite Adversity

Succeeding Despite Adversity

Your ability to be productive for your employer determines your value in the work place. When you can no longer produce or contribute toward the company's profit margin, you become a liability. A person who provides a service or produces a product is a producer. A parent who works to provide for the family is a producer. Producers have given us the electric light bulb, discovered blood plasma, and invented the street lights. There is a producer in nearly every home, community and city. These winners leave their homes daily to provide for their families in order to gain greater financial freedom and to meet the demands of life. Producers are givers because their efforts make it possible for us to live better and more comfortably. As a producer, if you are not satisfied with your income, the way to increase it is to serve more people.

For the most part, society does not pick the role you play in this world. Society prefers that a producer with a positive attitude produce the results to serve humanity in a productive manner. Any positive way you choose to help people is a valuable asset. Whether or not you accept the statement, "I am a producer" does not exclude you from the fact that you are to some degree. Everyone is producing something in this world. What you produce reflects your life's conditioning which is influenced by your attitude and controlled by your thoughts.

Your productivity is rated by society by virtue of its demand. If you produce nothing with your time, then your productivity value to society is zero. Employers like to hire people with experience or individuals who are willing to learn. Their experience saves the employer money because training time is reduced.

Your system of virtues impacts society through your actions. Society decides whether your actions produce something beneficial. Our free enterprise system is based on a service to mankind through producing goods or providing services. If you aren't producing goods or providing a service, then you are taking from society. When society is responsible, it pays you for what you have contributed. However, if you labor as a lawbreaker, your efforts are outside of the laws of the land and you will be punished.

Producers are the source of the products or services that we enjoy everyday; their work gets results. You can count on producers to keep their word; they are people who are goal oriented. They are servers. A football quarterback who throws the winning pass, and a father or mother who provides for his or her families are examples of producers.

All of the heroes and people that we admire from our history were producers. The great ones from our history created thought pictures in their minds that they were determined to see happen. What they visualized in their imagination is what we're experiencing now. To them, the visualization process was like watching a television program concerning images of their dreams. The image on the television program represents the thought picture—the vision of their dreams. They took action on their ideas and went out and became productive.

Family Meeting Needs

When I speak of needs, I am not thinking about being in a state of need. I believe that all rational needs we want are possible. When you take the focus off what is lacking in your life and focus only on desired possibilities, the world of possibilities will become your reality. In the reality in which we exist, you can meet your needs; all you have to do is apply yourself. Applying yourself might mean getting a job or earning a technical or college education.

In America, a baby comes into the world without the basic

necessities of clothes and other needs. However, a baby's needs are met first by parents and later in life by the individual. Needs are the basic necessities a person requires. Your needs are many but among them are food, clothes, and shelter. "I need water," said the stranded man in the desert. If you rescued this man, those would be his words. He would be truthful in what he is asking for. However, we are not in a desperate situation as in this illustration. If you let your needs go unattended, you'll find yourself in a desperate position. You have to be disciplined enough to do the right thing first, which is to take care of your needs. Your needs are much more important than going "off on a tangent" seeking pleasure for the moment.

Sometimes you may allow friends to influence you into doing the things they want instead of what you may want to do. When this happens, you will notice that it sets you into a failure mode. You must stop and determine that you will take care of your needs first. If you were in an accident, stranded and pinned down inside a wrecked car on a hot day, you would no doubt be thirsty. Besides getting your superficial wounds attended to and getting freed from the crash site, water is the only other thing you need at the moment. You noticed that while you were trapped, your lips became parched and chapped. The intense heat from the sun caused your tongue to crack, swell and blister. You don't wish to have water or want it, you must have it! If the opportunity presents itself, you will do what it takes to get a drink of water—that's a need.

Wants are the things you wish to acquire, but they are not a top priority. After the basic needs of most people have been satisfied, they should satisfy what they want next. When I was young, I wanted a bicycle for Christmas. I had no idea that I would get it; I just told my parents to tell Santa Claus to get it for me. I was a kid, and at Christmas time it seemed that all things were possible. I already had toys, (most of them I made myself) but I wanted something new, a bicycle. When Christmas came around, I was overwhelmed with joy because I had gotten what I wanted.

The bicycle that I got for Christmas was a want and not a need. I wanted that bike so badly that my parents got it for me. It was something I wanted, which came after my parents made sure that I had food, clothes, and shelter. The principle here is that your basic needs take precedence over the things you want.

These needs take precedence over shopping, partying, and drinking. Your basic needs should come first.

Concern, Consistency and Edification

Most organizations, businesses and educational systems operate from mission statements, rules or guidelines. These instruments are used to ensure that the whole organization operates alike. Being concerned and consistent are the way these organizations try to operate. The best way for the public to view the consistency of organizations is to visit fast food chains in different locations. You will notice that their mode of operation is virtually the same; they are consistent. In order to get employers to focus on the values of being concerned, consistent, and edifying, the employees have to be willing to encourage, to support, and to help the company remain true to its mission statement.

Edification means to improve or buildup a person. When you talk to employees who believe in the corporate culture, these people will edify the company. All you need to do is to ask them about the company's goods or services and you will be pleasantly surprised to hear them edify the company. Being concerned, consistent and edifying are an excellent blend in organizations—the blend also works wonders in the home.

The home is the one place parents should take the opportunity to introduce children to the benefits of being concerned, consistent, and edifying. Parents aren't selling their children products or services; instead, they are encouraging their children to abide by their rules, values and virtues. In order for parents to make consistency, edification, and concern work in their homes they have to be diligent in administering their home rules.

Parents have to edify each other in the presence of their children. To be effective with rearing children, they must speak with one voice—support each other. If the household consists of a single parent, the parent has to ensure that the children are consistent in abiding by the house rules. Additionally, the single parent should see to it that the children edify the benefits of respecting the parent's rules, virtues, values, and dreams for their success.

Family Value Structure

As a design engineer, I was taught to design a structure strong enough to operate under normal conditions as well as worst case scenarios. My designs were given parameters, which determined their limits. The engineering systems which I designed were produced to earn a profit. When designing for the clients, consideration was given for budget, heat dissipation, space limitations, incompatibility of metals, ease of use, quality, and other factors. Also, as professionals, we were responsible for arriving to work on time, handling our work load, and maintaining a professional appearance. Every prosperous person, event or organization has as its foundation a structured system that leads to success.

The family is the basic structure for society. In the family, a child should be taught a belief and value structure strong enough to handle normal life skills as well as competent enough to handle worst case scenarios. The family is a formula for success because it is a place for the youth to be shaped and molded. Single parents, legal guardians and extended families are all examples of successful families. Your original potential to procreate and start a family begins with a male and female and ends with children. You fulfill the original potential best in a two-parent family structure. The mother and father in a two-parent relationship can *each* possibly contribute 100 per cent parental love, educational support, a sense of stability, self-esteem development, and family virtues to the children. My father was not a part of my life while I was young; however, my stepfather provided an adequate two-parent model for the children in our family. Good family virtues and beliefs are what give structure to a youth's life. Parents are the example that the youth sees first as a model. Children trust their parents and depend on them to meet their needs. They model their parents' example. They learn to interact socially with people and to gain important values from the family.

Family Value Fence

Values are highly thought of and important to you. Your values can be abstract or material, but they are given their personal worth only by you. The things that you value will keep you busy.

Parents can instill values in the lives of youth by letting them see it active or manifested in their lives. The youth will notice the benefits and rewards for making a certain value a part of his or her life. More importantly, the youth learns by your example. When the value of being an example for your children is understood, you will respect the notion that you have to possess a value in order to duplicate it in another person's life.

A fence is an important part of the property of a home. As the front line of defense, you hope the fence will act as a boundary to limit children or animals from leaving the property and to protect the home by restricting it from intruders. The values you believe in are like the nails which are driven into the boards to secure and attach the fence together. To develop a strong value fence for their children, parents need to cultivate positive attributes in them.

The value fence instills positive core beliefs, virtues, and attitudes a family believes. Children want to know and to feel that they are loved and that there are limits. These limits encourage children to respect their parents, thus allowing parents to "train the child in the way he should go." Where there is no love, there is no respect. Teach children respect and it will be returned to you.

Parents want their children to obey their rules so that they will later obey the laws of society. As children grow, parents may have to prop them up from time to time to make sure that they stay within their value fence. Often, children will test you to see how far their limits are apart. Some parents set their limits too closely. Perhaps, you have noticed children who have lived a sheltered life. Their limits were too close. These children grow up living their lives moving forward with their feet on the brakes. The children's every move is overwhelmed by doubt, negative thinking and fear. These children were never given the opportunity to develop confidence in themselves. Conversely, some parents set their limits too far apart. Children are allowed to stay out late with whomever they desire. This is not good because they grow up believing that they can do anything they are big enough to do. They do not understand boundaries.

Parents should explain to children their "value boundaries," or "value fence;" so that, if they wander over to its extremities (value boundaries) they will want to return. A value fence (family values) will help them to learn a sense of independence, a regard for human life, and a self-supporting attitude. Because there are benefits to this life-style, obeying the laws of society produces good, law abiding citizens.

CHARACTER BENCHMARK: LESSON # 11

Family Wisdom and
Clarification Lessons on Morality

In a time when both parents or single parents are working, it is difficult to see that all of the positive values are passed on to the children. However, it is incumbent upon you to ensure that your virtues are passed on to your children, regardless of the work or social constraints that bind you. What you have to keep in mind is that your children are your future and that the reason you are working is to provide for them physically, spiritually, intellectually and emotionally. Every life is a miracle and a blessing; each life should be treated with love and respect.

The following six tales or stories are formatted to spark or "jump-start" a dialogue with youth. Additionally, they are to be used to help individuals clarify and disseminate positive values or beliefs on various topics covered.

Family Dialogue Lesson # 1: A Talk with Mom and Dad

One cold winter afternoon Mom and Dad called me over to sit with them around the fireplace. The fire was dancing, seemingly with joy to be in the midst of the logs.

It was fine with me because all I was doing was watching the weather having its way outside my window. The trees had no leaves. The snow seemed to be attracted to any surface that didn't have a white blanket of snow on it, yet. The pond was nearly frozen over and just about ready for ice skating. I noticed birds flying, which amazed me, especially given the almost frigid weather.

I was puzzled as to why my parents called me and had no idea what they wanted to discuss. I thought maybe it was a review of the "birds and bees" story. Maybe this was the time for me to show more responsibility than I had shown in the past.

Dad called me over and said, "Son, you know that we are strong believers in God." I acknowledged that I realized they were believers. And mom said, "But son, there are some additional things we wish to discuss with you other than what we have talked about in the past."

Dad said, "Our family has a tradition, a set of family values, which has always caused us to prosper in the world. The reason this has been true is mainly because of our spiritual beliefs, and our willingness to serve a lot of people. Our parents have always passed down their values by having discussions with the children. We learned what difficulties life might present which could lead us off the path of our dreams. "By letting you know ahead of time our values regarding something we believe, you will be prepared to face barriers properly in the future. Son, there are twelve concepts that we want to cover with you this evening. These will not be the only ones that we will talk about, but this will give us a start. We believe in success, and we believe that you believe in success, also. The following are important for you to know." Complete the following sentence stems by discussing them:

1. Never be content with taking the path of least resistance *because...*
2. You should always be patriotic toward your country *because...*
3. Always have pride in everything that you do because...
4. Develop your social skills because your main purpose in life will be centered around how you will serve others *because...*
5. You should be willing to call most of your "shots." An independent thinker does this *because...*
6. Like a tree that survives because it bends in a storm, you must be flexible at times when it does not conflict with your core virtues *because...*

7. "Birds of a feather flock together," in this case what we are talking about is character. Make sure you choose peers with character *because...*
8. You should be dependable in life *because...*
9. We believe that the best birth control is abstinence *because...*
10. You have always observed me respecting your mother and other women. You, too, must respect your mother and people of the opposite gender *because...*
11. Your heritage is your strength regardless of how others have portrayed it *because...*
12. My parents always told us kids to stick together, believe in God and get an education *because...*

Family Dialogue Lesson #2: Programming the New Computer

Two honor students, Sue and Tim, in the Human Relations 102 class were asked to program a new computer system. Their supervisor wanted Sue and Tim to define moral concepts to create software parameters so that the computer will be able to differentiate between morality and immorality. So, they input ten concepts and pressed enter. Seconds later, the computer responded with questions. To give accurate information, they reflected on what had been taught to them by their professors. They keyed in the new information and pressed enter. Moments later, the computer replied. Complete the following sentence stems by discussing them:

1. You should always have good "work habits," *because...*
2. I believe in having "faith," in God *because...*
3. This country was built on "courage," you have that heritage *because...*
4. I think a person who "keeps his or her word," is truthful and dependable *because...*
5. I want you to "get a good education," *because...*
6. You honor your employer when you "have good work habits," *because...*
7. People who get things done are those with a "positive attitude," *because...*

8. It is important to have faith in "God?" *because...*
9. It is important that you not use "illegal drugs" such as marijuana *because...*
10. Good "friendship," is more valuable than money *because...*

After the computer had stored in memory its responses it said, "thank you." The computer could understand all of the concepts with one exception—it could not comprehend drug abuse.

Family Dialogue Lesson # 3:
Teaching the English Language Course

One summer you volunteer to teach English to immigrants in order for them to earn their citizenship. Your new students do not understand a word of English.

You select ten topics from the manual to cover with them. It delights you to watch the interest on their faces as you speak the words and statements. You pronounce the first word and the first fellow tries to say the word imitating your accent. The group manages to pronounce a few phrases on each topic.

You feel you need to dismiss the class today in order to get some clarification on some other concepts that came up in the discussion. You reflect on what has been taught by mentors or you discuss them with your parents. The next day, other questions come up. Complete the following sentence stems by discussing them:

1. You should build positive "self worth" *because...*
2. You should always "have respect for yourself" at all times *because...*
3. You should be willing to "make right choices" with small matters *because...*
4. Marriage is the best time to "engage in sexual intercourse" *because...*
5. You can increase your "self-esteem" by believing in yourself *because...*
6. You should learn the consequences and dangers of smoking" *because...*
7. Believing in truth" will always be an asset in life *because...*
8. Too much television viewing adversely affects you *because...*

9. I am not a "bigot" because I *believe ...*
10. I should believe in "being responsible" *because...*

Family Dialogue Lesson # 4: A Visit to Grandparent's House

One summer you go to visit your grandparents on the farm for a month. Your grandparents want to do some special things for your thirteenth birthday. They plan to take you camping, to the amusement park, to the movies, and to the zoo. They, also, plan to take you for walks in the beautiful countryside of the farm.

They explain to you that there are concerns grandparents in your family have always selected to cover with each grandchild. Based on their concerns and how these concerns may effect your life-style, they said, "We want to help you with this mid-stage passage into adulthood."

With her beautiful patented smile, Grandma begins to speak. She starts by giving you a sheet of paper with nine concepts that she wants to discuss with you. Complete the following sentence stems by discussing them:

1. If you have "negative thinking," you become limited *because...*
2. You should show "leadership," in your life *because...*
3. You should "avoid teen pregnancy," because you should not...
4. I "love" you *because...*
5. There are a few things you can do to "protect yourself," from crime and they are *because...*
6. Which form of employment has the greatest appeal: owning a business or working for someone else? *I prefer ...*
7. You should be over 15 years of age before you start to date *because...*
8. You should be committed to a moral life-style in spite of the many youthful detractions *because...*
9. You need to be aware of the AIDS virus and how to protect yourself *because...*

At this point, you walk to their big pond. Looking at the pond, you realize that this is one of your favorite places. The fish are splashing in the water while the turtles are poking their heads above the water for air. The sun is shining brightly, causing the water to produce a reflection. The birds make their special sounds as they fly off flapping their beautiful wings. Granddaddy motions you to stop and sit on a log in the shade near the water. He says to you, "On this paper are the nine topics I want to discuss." Complete the following sentence stems by discussing them:

1. You can avoid "gangs," *because...*
2. You should have important dreams to accomplish in life *because...*
3. You should "never give up," *because...*
4. You should learn to set goals *because...*
5. You should use critical thinking in everyday living *because...*
6. You should have heroes and heroines *because...*
7. You should know how a vision differ from a dream *because...*
8. You should seek to be successful *because...*
9. You should understand barriers are a part of your success *because...*

Family Dialogue Lesson # 5: The Martians Have Landed!

Your work as a scientist requires you to attempt to make contact with alien beings. While working one day in the science laboratory after a tiring eight-hour stretch, you accidentally pressed a button that lowers the transmission signal. Under normal conditions, you would not have used this signal to try to make first contact with extraterrestrial beings.

The signal was active all night and when you returned to the office the next day, there was a message on the screen. Instantly, you realized that you had made contact with intelligent alien beings. After much excitement, you contacted your supervisor and later the President of the United States.

You were asked to tutor the Martians in our language and way of life in preparation for their visit to our world. The Martians were fast learners and looked forward daily to working a 20-hour tutorial work day. However, there were a few concepts that we discussed that puzzled them.

To be careful and to give accurate information, you wanted to defer the answers until the next day so you could discuss them with your colleagues. The next day, a response came back on your computer screen from some disappointed Martians. They wanted to work twenty hours today and they agreed to allow you to reply tomorrow. Next day, you keyed in the information and pressed enter. You are prepared today to answer their questions because the Martians were eager for answers to their many questions. Complete the following sentence stems by discussing them:

1. What does the Biblical phrase "fruit of the spirit" means? *It means ...*
2. What does the term "serving" means? *It means ...*
3. Why does racism exist in the world? *It means ...*
4. What does the phrase "self-respect" means? *It means ...*
5. What does the word "discipline" means? *It means ...*
6. What does the phrase "having a good character" means? *It means ...*
7. Why is being a good employee important? *It means ...*
8. Who are givers? *It means ...*
9. Who are takers? *It means ...*

The Martians seemed to be satisfied with your answers. They checked their schedules and decided that they would visit in 239 years. Because the average Martian's life span is 5000 years, they were unaware of our short life span. You had to explain to them that humans don't live that long. With some encouragement, you were able to get them to commit to visiting right away—in five years.

Family Dialogue Lesson # 6:
Lenell Geter Speaks to Parents and Mentors

I had just concluded my banquet speech with the statement, "Our children are our future, so treat them as if they are important." I was about to speak to someone at the head table, when a satisfied group of parents and mentors surrounded me.

The first to ask questions were parents having problems with their son. The father stated, "If my son doesn't stop abusing drugs, I fear he will be arrested for distribution of illegal drugs." These parents seemed to be burdened, because not only did their son have the drug problem, he was also an angry child. The child seemed to always choose inappropriate ways to handle conflicts.

I asked the parents to discuss with me how they handled their son's problems in the past. With quite a bit of prompting, utilizing psycho-cultivation, I became satisfied with our new approach. I suggested that they go home and get along with their son. I suggested they have the boy talk until he desires to stop. Then, ask a few questions to let him know that they were listening. Next, I suggested that they allow him to talk some more. When he is finished, let him know how much you love him. Discuss and clarify your values and principles with him on any topic he chooses. Let him know that it is the goal of your discussion for him to become a successful citizen.

I admonished the parents neither to "holler" at their son nor to "talk down" to him, but to treat him the way they would want to be treated. I listened to the way they planned to approach their son; they planned to include several important points in their discussion. Complete the following sentence stems by discussing them:

1. I want you to view avoiding illegal drugs and physical conflicts as being mentally strong *because...*
2. If you find yourself about to buy illegal drugs don't *because...*
3. Everyone must seek meaningful employment *because...*
4. When you feel rejected by friends, peers or family, realize that they are not rejecting you. They are rejecting your choices *because...*
5. Illegal drug "Associations cause people to assimilate;" You become like the people you associate with *because...*

CHAPTER 11

Building Moral Character

Exposure to Moral Character, Virtues, and Positive Life Experiences

In order to encourage moral character in a youth, the youth has to see the virtues existing in the lives of those in the youth's home. Children get their first exposure to character education from their parents' home. You teach them right from wrong and how to give instead of how to take. It all should start in the home.

The next place a youth gets moral teaching is in your house of worship. At the age of one or two years old, youths can't comprehend the religious experience, but they are being "trained up" by your example until they are able to be taught with understanding.

When children leave the home to start the first grade, they enter school with your moral character teaching. If you have done a good job, your child will respect the rights of others, respect authority, and behave with dignity and self-respect. When children are behaving outside of normal standards, their behavior reveals what was lacking in their home training. When there are constant disciplinary problems in school, other children are not learning and are being affected by the student creating the problems. Therefore, to continue to reinforce moral character, you have to place children in life experiences that will continue to emphasize virtue.

One of the best life experiences that continues to reinforce excellence in character is being exposed to the virtues of the Boys or Girls Scouts. When I was a boy scout, the first thing my scout troop leader had me study was the character of a boy scout from the scouts handbook. At the scout meetings, all of the scouts would stand and pledge allegiance to the flag of the United States of America. While we were still standing, we recited the virtues of the Boy Scouts which made me proud of what a scout is. These are the words we recited, "A boy scout is trustworthy, loyal, helpful, friendly, courteous, kind, obedient, cheerful, thrifty, brave, clean and reverent." I recall, fondly, the valuable life training that I received from Troop 137 Boy Scouts in Denmark, South Carolina. I liked the uniforms, the water canteen, the back pack, the compass, camping and hiking.

Additionally, exposure to the world through reading books, listening to tapes, and traveling, is a great opportunity to enrich the lives of children. The best way for parents to teach their children to become readers are to read to them and to let them see them reading. If you don't encourage these kinds of things, your children will not commit to investing their interest in education. When your children become readers, this is the time to give them simple inspirational books and books on moral lessons.

Finally, youths need to have athletic activities, musical activities, and employment activities *(see Appendix B for 100 Activities for Youth Success and Character Development)*, that will give them engaging things to focus on. What you focus on will become attractive for you to do. If children are not given productive things to do, they will find nonproductive things to do. You have probably come to realize youths are abusing drugs, becoming sexually active, joining gangs and becoming apathetic toward school. For these reasons, parents must start exposing children early to situations where they can learn character, virtues and values.

CHARACTER BENCHMARK: LESSON # 12

20 Essentials of a Youth's Character and Self-esteem Development

People who are law abiding citizens produce goods and provide services that benefit others. Doctors, business owners, farmers, lawyers, etc., are all considered producers because they give back to society. The people whose actions fall outside the laws of society detract from the community. They fail to eliminate their negative thoughts and multiply their positive ones. They take from the lives of people and become non-producers as a result. Through repetition, their negative thinking patterns keep them nonproductive unless they are willing to change their beliefs.

We need to cultivate in the youth's mind respect for the laws of the land. Too many youngsters are willing to take a chance with their future by breaking the law. Character, self-discipline and personal accountability are keys for having respect for the law.

Successful living within the law means that you understand the laws, accept them and abide by them. Your undertakings are carried out with respect for the law. These laws require that people live their lives in this circle of rules called laws. Our thoughts to become law abiding citizens can be driven by us or our negative thoughts can control us. In the animal world, animals are concerned with procreation, food, and shelter. People also are concerned with these things. They have learned to bypass these basic instinctive needs to develop the power of their minds. The tools that they have invented have gone a long way toward improving their environment. Technology has increased our ability to track the speed of drivers on the highway. It has enabled us to use remote surveillance cameras to protect our homes and property. With all of this technology, we are sometimes at a loss to protect our youth from the vices of the streets.

I was in my mid-20s when I first met my father, a businessman. He said something profound to me. It was, "What we teach in the home should be stronger than what is taught in the street." He was alluding to the power of teaching the Word of God in the home so as to strengthen children and protect them from succumbing to the influence of street life.

I realized that my mother and stepfather had reared us children using this concept. Because of the values I learned at home, I was morally strong enough to resist the street life. Now, I do not hold anything against my biological father for not being by my side all of those years, though I wish he would have called or visited, periodically, when I was growing up. However, thanks to my mother, stepfather, and the strong extended family relationships, I was able to live a balanced life. I decided that when I started my family, I would be there for my children.

It is important that you use moral values as your bedrock from which you build your children's character foundation as you teach them the twenty essentials of character education and self-esteem development. For your family discussions and implementation, I would suggest the following values for starters: *self-discipline, self-improvement, productive work attitude, faith, respect, love, justice, truth, patience, reliability, friendship, and kindness.* I will not define these virtues or values in this book, as I think they are prerequisites and would be best served for the family to discuss and define them with their children. However, after teaching these virtues in the home, next discuss the twenty essentials to improve their self-image, knowledge of culture, character, and relationship with others.

These essentials which, I believe, are important to every youth's or adult's self-esteem development. Although I did not learn all of these concepts at once in the home, I learned some of them from reading, in lectures, and from observation. Life taught me the rest. I'm going to discuss twenty character essentials; however, there may be more.

Essential #1:
Family Virtues and Values Clarification

Families need to have a set of virtues that they want to guide their lives and the lives of their children. These values should be taught to their children just as they are able to talk. Once you have defined your family virtues, parents should make sure that these virtues are applied to all of the things they value. Officially, my family did not define our virtues; however, they were defined by their life-style. My mother taught her children to live a just life as in the Biblical "fruits of the spirit," When I was going through my "Texas Nightmare," I relied constantly on the virtues of "the fruits of the Spirit" to remind me of my spiritual character. I realized the kind of person I am. One of the fruits of the spirit was long suffering, which caused me to be patient and to have self-control.

Values are the concepts and principles a family believes in, such as getting a good education or having a solid career. Parents need to be able to sit down with their children and discuss their values and virtues on any topic that comes up. Most conflicts arise because the family fails to communicate their values to children at an early age. When they begin to talk, you should demonstrate them. For example, if you want to teach children to clean, then model the activity by cleaning yourself.

Have you ever been asked to do something and when you did, you found out to your dismay that there was a communication problem? The communication problem prevented you from getting the results that you were expecting. Well, this is what happens when you fail to clarify your values and virtues with your children.

Often some families have a problem discussing topics like sex with their children. They use vague language when discussing these topics with them. The youth ends up with information that is vague and confusing, at best. If you want your children to learn the truth about a subject such as sex, you need to clarify it with them before they learn about it in the streets. Sit down with them with all of the resource materials that are pertinent for them.

Essential #2:
Living Life by "Example"

In the *Building Youth Character Through Self-development* course that I teach in the school systems as a part of my program, we take the classes on a prison tour. The tour is not designed to be a "scare" tactic, but to be informative and educational about choices, consequences and making quality decisions. On one of the inmate tours, a guide was giving his testimony on how a life of disobedience and crime landed him into prison. He said, "We don't need any more role models and mentors. We need community examples." Maybe he felt that "role models" and "mentors" sometimes practice hypocrisy. "People need to be good community examples to follow," he said. As a community example, people need to be willing to live the life of a provider, a community worker, or good parents.

You are just dad or mom to your children, and they see the example you set around the house. By teaching a child to live by example, you are also encouraging values like truthfulness and character. Parents can best teach their virtues by living their lives as community examples. For instance, when you ask your child to do something, say "thank you." By saying "thank you," you are indirectly teaching your child to duplicate your response. This concept is teaching by example. This whole idea of living your life by example, not a person playing a role, a role model, or a mentor can become effective in all areas of life, especially with smoking, drinking, and education.

Essential #3:
Value of Education

We need to pass on to our next generation the value of an education. All of the advancements in our society happened because a person with a formal education or the self-educated decided to make something positive happen. A good education should include books written by experienced achievers whether they are academic or motivational. There should be special emphasis placed on books that are motivational because these books are used to improve the person's attitude and self-esteem. These books are often found in the library or bookstore in the self-help, motivational or inspirational section. My first inspirational book was the Bible. From the Bible I learned about faith, reaping and sowing, work, and dignity.

The focus on academic books should not be diminished because they help to develop the person's career interests. My academic interests have provided for me a career that allows me to pursue my dreams.

Essential #4:
Cultural and Identity Awareness

Every child needs to be taught the importance their ancestor's culture played in this world. I can't think of a people on this planet whose culture has not affected the world in a positive way at one time. Sure there are times and situations where that same group of people's ancestor's actions were less than honorable. However, pride in one's culture benefits the youth who are looking for heroes.

Youths get a great deal of their pride, self-esteem and identity from their culture. When children believe that they represent value, this belief will often transform them into good citizens. Parents need to invest time each month in their child's life in order to ensure that their child has a positive identity. Take time to draw a family tree for your children. Teach them their family history. Show them the ones who succeeded using hard work, persistence and dedication.

Essential #5: Spirituality and Righteousness

Everyone has some type of belief or non-belief in God. I happen to believe in God. There are many people who don't believe in God or they doubt the existence of God. My spiritual belief system was cultivated from an early age. It was not uncommon to hear my mother or grandmother use statements of praise to God while carrying out their chores. My family believed in attending church. We were members of Mt. Zion Baptist Church, but we attended Rome Baptist Church because it was within walking distance.

When I was involved in the "Texas Nightmare," I was forced into a hostile environment where I could have gotten hurt any day. I remember long periods of meditation, prayers and claiming or believing. Claiming or believing is a conviction that the promises in the Scriptures pertinent to the situation at hand is evident that, as a child of God, your prayers will be answered.

Through all of my emotional ups and downs, I landed on solid ground because of my spiritual connection. My life moved from an environment of freedom to an environment of imprisonment. Although I had possessions, friends, money and God, it was God that I believed turned the tide which led to my release.

Essential #6:
Positive Peers

Every child has to make the decision to follow virtues which were instilled by family members or by default to follow the values of friends or strangers. Each time two people get together, the one with the strongest leadership ability, whether good or evil, will overshadow the other. That's why teaching your children the way they should go should be your goal.

When I was young, my parents taught me many positive attributes I should look for in choosing my peers. These positive attributes were meant to apply in all areas of my life as I dealt with people: such as sports, work, family, religion, school, etc. My mother worked to instill a desire for education, work, honesty, and character in us. The eight of us were expected to associate with positive peers who mirrored our virtues.

Essential #7:
Employment

A farmer went to the farm supply store and purchased some grain. He cultivated the soil of his farm and planted some seeds. The seeds grew quickly and produced so much crop that the farmer was able to sell some at the market. With the profits from the sale of the grain, he was able to purchase more grain, to give to charity, and to save. This is an example of a producer producing a product that serves other people. This type of sowing and reaping has been in effect for thousands of years.

In modern times, we sow by becoming an employee or by owning a business. We are bartering our talents or skills in exchange for money. Like the farmer, with the money we can do many things for our families. As a youth, my first big job was the work I did for a local doctor. I earned $40 dollars a week, which was a lot of money during that time. With this money, I was able to acquire some of the things that I wanted.

Essential #8:
Understanding the Law

Society has its own values called laws. We must abide by these laws or suffer the consequences. To ensure that the laws are followed, society made provisions for law enforcement of its values.

Our form of government is called a democracy, and in a democracy the people appoint a person to represent them, called the President, who is the chief executive officer in our government. The House of Representatives and the Senate, called The Congress of the United States, are the legislative bodies of government. Congress is responsible for making the laws that govern our lives.

In the United States, we are free to pursue any career our hearts desire. We can set out to become a millionaire or just maintain our current income level. With money, we can go out into the marketplace and purchase any goods and services our hearts desire. It all starts with a dream, which is something deep down that pulls you toward what you want.

I heard on the radio that a couple of young men tried to steal or "car-jack" an expensive BMW automobile from its owners. The owners were not injured in the mishap. The crime occurred because the "carjackers" lacked a constructive vision. A vision teaches you to work until your dreams become a reality. Normally, we would work and earn money to purchase the BMW. However, the carjackers wanted it fast and easy. However, to acquire the BMW, the process starts with a mental thought picture where the car is claimed as a dream to pursue. Next, you make personal changes in your life that will allow you to qualify for employment that pays more money. Then the dream is transformed into a goal when it becomes specific. The goal is pursued until it is obtained. That is how you obtain a BMW!

The problem arises when the youth uses his external vision and goes out and takes the BMW. Instead, the youth should have created an internal vision and made the personal changes needed to pursue his dream. He tried to take the object of his gratification. He was not willing to delay his extreme desire for the BMW and in the end he did not receive the gratification sought after.

The law is designed to serve you. It is intended to prevent others from abridging your rights to freedom, justice and the pursuit of happiness. Our families and their children need to take some time off and visit our nation's capital, their state capital, and talk with the representatives from their district and question them on the law. Also, visit the police station, talk to the chief of police, and talk to the mayor and the city council persons so as to better understand the laws. When people get to know how the law serves them, there will be a greater respect for the law.

Essential #9: Learning One's Purpose

I stated in an earlier chapter that I pursued the meaning of, "what is life's purpose?" You have skills that are unique to you, you are unique, and your purpose here on planet earth is unique and special. In all of my studies, I have found that people's true purposes are to serve themselves and others, which suggests that we need each other.

I have watched ants march about carrying crumbs of bread. They seem to have no conflict as they carry out the master plan of the colony, which is to serve in the propagation of the species. Even on this level, the act of servicing is manifested.

Our true purpose is to serve. Our talents should be improved so as to enrich the lives of others by serving a multitude of people. Look at your many assets, skills and abilities and decide what is it you want to do with your life. Once you have decided what it is you want to accomplish, make the vision as detailed as possible. Select a dream out of that vision and pursue it with well-defined and specific goals.

Once you have determined your dream, do what is necessary to accomplish them. When a personal dream is decided, there should also be a collateral dream to benefit others. If a group of owners have a company manufacturing bicycles, their dream will provide not only for themselves but others. In this example, the employees get to earn a living for their efforts because of the owner's foresight to manifest a dream. The consumer gets to purchase and enjoy the bicycle. And the owners, who took the risk to start the business, get to reap the benefits of their hard work and effort.

Essential #10: Handling Adversity

One of the most comforting Scriptures for me is Romans 8:28 which reads, "And we know that all things work together for good to those who love God, to those who are called according to His purpose." The way we view adversities is sometimes misunderstood.

Adversities should be thought of as being experiences that occur from time to time in our lives. These experiences always have a benefit associated with them. In order to handle these adversities, your "spiritual-self" must be "turned on." The "spiritual-self" which consists of your thought deposits manifests itself in your character, morals and faith. These deposits are attributes that are needed in order for you to handle adversities successfully.

A person of character will stick to his or her convictions throughout the test of time or the difficulties of the circumstances. This person is consistent in his or her deeds and actions. You can trust a person with character, because the person is usually honest.

When people have good moral deposits, they will be able to discern between right and wrong. Often, when a depraved person commits some heinous crime, the individual is using a selfish sense of morals. To these people, other people don't have a choice in their own life or liberty; they feel the need to decide the fate of others. These are the types of people who arbitrarily walk into a place and deliberately take the life of innocent people.

Faith is what we hope for. Our hope is based on the fact that God will assist in bringing our dreams and desires into reality. It's taking a step forward not knowing, other than with faith, whether the dream will take place.

Every success story has its adversities associated with it. There would not have been a success story had the person not achieved in spite of the adversities. The youth of the world have to understand that they don't have to turn to drinking alcohol or abusing drugs to solve their problems. They need only turn to God, by associating through prayer, reading the Scriptures, and living according to the Word.

Essential #11: Positive Attitude

If you have never met *can do* people you will. They are the kinds of people who believe that all things are possible. They believe that they can help design their own future. They know that they are a creation of God. God allows them the ability to be creative with their lives. They can use their creativity to carve out their future. If not, they will allow, by default, others to do it for them. They know that a rock was created by God. But humans view the rock's future as theirs to script and refine into a figure of their creativity.

After relocating to South Carolina, my friends Al Bah and Jackie Bah of Texas invited Marcia and me to hear Dexter Yager speak and to learn about his free enterprise business at a convention in Charlotte, North Carolina. At the convention, I received the largest dosage of positive attitude that I have every experienced. There were over 25,000 exuberant conventioneers in the Charlotte, North Carolina Coliseum and there were others in the overflow facilities.

We stepped in the coliseum to find that it was an electrifying experience. I realized later why they were so excited. Their excitement stemmed from the idea that they were happy for the successes of others, yet realized that the same success could be duplicated in their lives. Most of the entrepreneurs were there with their spouses to learn how to become financially free, to gain more time and freedom, to have more control over their future and to make life better for their children.

You have to find something in your life, such as the entrepreneurs did, that excites you to higher levels of accomplishment. Once you have found the dream that excites you, look for a vehicle that will help you accomplish those dreams. A positive attitude will usually accompany a person with a dream. A dreamer will tend to affirm people. They'll possess an upbeat attitude. Faith is a tool that they use to help in the pursuit of their dreams. As they believe and have faith, their circumstances change to reflect their attitude. A dreamer knows most input from other people that enters the unprotected mind will often be negative. On the other hand, to become positive in attitude, an individual has to associate with positive input through affirmations, reading or other people.

Essential #12: Delayed Gratification

Delayed gratification means to put off for later something that delights you or gives you pleasure. Discipline is at the core of delayed gratification. Whether we admit it or not, whatever an individual does is done to bring about some pleasure. To override instant gratification, you must have a big dream that will make you feel that it is unwise for you to seek pleasure before accomplishing the dream.

People who do something on the spur of the moment when it is clearly not in their best interest, have not learned how to put off for later something that they desire. They are lacking in understanding to the extent that they allow their emotional and physical desires to overtake their judgment.

A flower shows its beauty as an expression of its glory. Humans express themselves in a variety of ways, such as singing, public speaking and interacting with people. In learning to delay your gratification, your emotions are not the best representatives of your best judgment.

In this hypothetical example, we get to see how Tom and Tisa handle their problem with delayed gratification. Tom is the head of the household and works hard to provide for his wife and five children each week. He lives in a rented house and they have only one car in the household. Tom's wife Tisa, works hard on a minimum wage job. Both parents often work long hours of overtime to make ends meet. They live in a constant state of argument over money that is being wasted mostly due to Tom's abuse of alcohol.

Tom drinks alcohol heavily; at least once a month he wastes all of his paycheck at the bar drinking. He comes home drunk, to the grief of his family. The whole family suffers during these episodes and Tisa ends up battered each month by Tom. Tom is harming his body and his dignity, as well as setting a poor "example" for his children. The children are "latch key children" and are often left at home because both parents work. The children watch uncensored movies, stay out late and are rearing themselves.

Tom is currently functioning in a physical and emotional mode because he mainly serves the needs of the body. He is not doing anything to improve his intellectual and 'spiritual self'. His home environment is not a fight or flee situation which would warrant such physical action, but Tom has not graduated to a higher relationship with his wife Tisa.

His body is addicted to the drug alcohol and, while under its influence, his judgment is impaired. Because his judgment is impaired, he cannot effectively delay his gratification. He is a servant to his emotions as well as to his addiction.

Had Tom operated at the intellectual mode, he could have, at best, relied on his logic, willpower, virtues or positive attitude to sway him. Yet the intellectual mode can be compromised, changed or altered by others, thus weakening his resolve. The physical and emotional mode can still cancel out the intellectual mode of expression.

What I recommend is a blend of all three of these behavioral modes, the biggest portion of the three going to the spiritual mode. When the focus is on the "spiritual-self," it removes the desire for you to be a servant to the body, to the intellect and to the emotional behavioral modes. The focus of delayed gratification is to place emphasis on helping others and serving God.

Serving God has the power to bring love, morality and hope to millions of people. When people really believe that they are following the benevolent will of God, their actions are consistent with the attitude of love. Love serves God, one's self and humanity. When people are filled with love, they will serve their families and others. By serving their families and others, they abandon the desire for instant gratification. They will be producers, meeting their family's needs, respecting life, and harming no one.

Essential #13:
Dreams and Goals

Your vision houses all of your dreams. The vision includes all of your little dreams and goals. When you decide on one thing it becomes a dream. It is taken off your vision landscape and becomes activated in your conscience and actions.

A dream is that something that you feel you need so badly that you are willing to do whatever it takes to have it. When you wake up in the morning, you think about it, during work it's on your mind and just before you go to sleep, you think about it. The dream becomes so consuming that if the opportunity arises, and it's legal and ethical, you will overcome fear and adversities to make it happen.

The goal consists of small measured steps toward accomplishing the dream. These steps are indicators to alert you when you are getting near to accomplishing your desires. If you stray off the main path, they guide you and remind you why you are pursuing the dream. Whether you like setting goals or, by default, allow someone else to do it for you, you still are a goal setter, except you are a poor one. If you set zero goals, you will get zero results toward that goal.

Essential #14: Self-respect

The way you treat yourself shows how well you respect yourself. Often the same respect you have for yourself you will show toward others. When someone gives you a sincere compliment, do you say "thank you" or do you try to down play the compliment? All people like to be respected. Deep down they want to be regarded as equals.

The most effective way to teach respect is to demonstrate it in your dealings. The people around you will tend to respect what you respect and disrespect what you disrespect. Therefore, work to be an *example* of what you are trying to instill in the lives of others.

Essential #15: Physical Conflict Avoidance Skills

One step before an actual physical conflict is physical conflict avoidance. It is an attitude that you don't want to be engaged in a physical altercation with anyone. It is a small opportunity to skip the fight and start the communication process. Always remember, it takes two people to fight. If one person finds a way to avoid the fight, it might save someone from getting hurt. The following conflict avoidance opportunities may be helpful to you:

a. Before a fight starts, ask the other person if there is any thing we can do to sit down and talk about this.

b. Relate to the person, get on his or her side, especially if you can understand why the person may feel this way.
c. Say, "Knowing what I know now, I would have done it differently."
d. Ask, "If we were friends, would you allow me a chance to talk this over with you?"
e. If you can walk away from the fight, you must not fight.

Sometimes people don't want to fight, but their friends often encourage them to fight. The peer group tries to put your ego on the line and they want you to think fighting is the only way for you to save face. Instead of fighting, always offer the other person in the conflict a chance to get out of it.

Essential #16:
Grooming

When I was at South Carolina State University, Roy Smith was one of the students who always dressed immaculately. When he was seen walking to and from classes, he was dressed in a suit and tie with a briefcase in hand. He looked like a businessman and talked like one too. Years later, I ran across him and I was curious to know why he dressed that way in college. He said, "As a student, I had already read great books such as *Think and Grow Rich* by Napoleon Hill, and others which cultivated a positive attitude for me." These books taught him how to set goals and have dreams. He said, "So, I naturally started seeing myself as that professional that I would be upon graduation and in my career." He was right, he is now a successful entrepreneur, happily married, with a beautiful family.

Your grooming is a reflection of your degree of social conformity whether you buy only brand name clothing; whether you dress conservatively; or whether you keep up with latest fads. Some fads are worn to shock the observer. Having the underwear showing and skimpy dressing are designed to draw attention to the wearer and to show indifference to tradition. In the business world, employers are looking for someone to fit into the corporate environment with their employees and clients. Thus, the dress will be more conservative. If your attitude of indifference continues into adulthood, then there will be little relatable qualities in you to fit in the corporate structure.

Essential #17: Consequences and Abuse

Every time you make a decision, consequences result from that decision. This happens because of the "law of cause and effect." The cause is the reason why something was done, and the effect is the outcome. If you set a goal to buy a car, and you work hard and you purchase it. The reason you wanted the car was the cause or reason for your actions, and the final possession of the car is the effect or rewarded.

Consequences are the effect of a decision already made. Consequences can also be the abuse of a deed or action. What this means, is that, what you did is what you get as a result of an earlier decision. If you abuse drugs, an irresponsible cause, and you get caught, the effect, you could go to prison. Or, if you live life responsibly, a responsible cause, your life-style will bear witness that you are responsible — the effect is a prosperous life-style.

Hundreds of teenagers are killed yearly because they decided to abuse alcohol and drive. Underage drinking is a serious matter and teenagers should not drink alcohol. There are responsibilities that go with consuming alcohol, even for an adult.

Essential #18: Patriotism

I am proud of my country! This should be the words of a person's feelings about the country he or she lives in. I happen to be a proud citizen of the United States of America. My patriotism is toward this country, the land of opportunity.

Whether forced into slavery or sold, many African American's ancestors came to America and were forced to live as slaves, but in Africa many were farmers, leaders and builders. The Africans came to this country with skills and talents. Their contributions helped to make America a great country! They became a painful part of America's history and a formula for its success. Yet, America could not have arrived so quickly at its level of greatness without the contribution of these Americans.

America is now willing to utilize the willing skills and talents of all of its people. Patriotism has influenced many people to make their country a better place to live. Everyone wants to live in a country where they can pursue their dreams and reap the fruits of their labor.

Although, there still exists racism and some social ills, we as a people are working to make things better. Patriotism starts with teaching youth by citing the positive things that people have contributed to their country. Teach them about the history of their country or state. Take them to their country's shrines. It would be patriotic to visit state and national capitols, parks, museums and monuments. It is imperative for Americans to visit the District of Columbia which contains many patriotic sites.

Essential #19: The Value of Work

The value of a person's work is determined by employers as wells as clients. To produce quality products, it helps if the employees enjoy the work that is entailed in producing the product or service. Because people enjoy their work, they will view the product or service as important. People place value on their work and that work reflects their personal standards regarding quality. Therefore, in order to keep the standards high, the owner of the business places a higher value on the work that his employees are doing.

I am sitting at my computer this Saturday having fun or, should I say, working. I would rather be doing something else, but I have as an ultimate goal to help people overcome adversities in their lives. This is my life's work, and because it is one of the things I enjoy doing, it brings me pleasure.

Working helps to bring value to your life. It reinforces the idea that you are responsible, an achiever, and a contributor to the world community. Working is a blessing to those who are able to do so.

Essential #20: Making a Difference

One of the best ways to make a difference is by volunteering to help someone. If you don't have money to give, you can give your time and effort. You can start by picking up the paper in your neighborhood. You can be a friend when someone loses a family member.

There are many ways you can make a difference in someone else's life. There are prisons, hospitals, and needy people who always need assistance. Your church or place of worship may have a soup kitchen for the homeless that needs volunteers.

CHARACTER BENCHMARK: LESSON # 13

13 Attributes of Work Character

Employers are willing to pay huge sums of money for training to improve the skills of a good employee. However, an employer is not willing to pay a penny for a potential employee who is without character. Cultivating and training new employees is a tremendous investment for the employer and they want people with character. Character is an attitude. The following thirteen attitudes are key character attributes employers are looking for in new employees.

Attribute #1:
Self-discipline

Self-discipline is self-control in your dealings with others. It is having the ability to conduct yourself without violating another person's rights. This attribute requires that you be able to submit yourself to authority or its rules.

Self-discipline produces a character pattern that is encouraged in society. It is an attitude that is acquired from associating with people who practice this behavior. In your home, parents must have a consistent method of encouraging self-discipline. The method starts with parents' behavior: if you want your children to live a disciplined life, you must live it first.

If a father is an alcoholic and he comes home drunk, his children learn from his behavior how to be out of control. Perhaps, he may tell his children that they should never drink alcohol because of what it has done to him. With some of his children this might work, but the others might become curious and try it thinking they can handle it.

It takes self-discipline to commit to having good character. We have free will, we have to decide daily to remain true to doing the right thing—that's character! Character is the consistency of our reputation that we have developed in the community or society. Your character is like having good credit. With good credit you can buy now and pay later. Based on your consistency in paying, creditors have decided that you pay your bills timely, and they don't mind doing business with you. Essentially, they are saying that you have self-discipline in paying your bills and your financial character or reputation is good. The way you build character is with truth and honesty. If your child finds, say a wallet, and he or she brings it to you, you should praise this act and you should try and find the owner. By praising this action and finding the owner, you are encouraging honesty, integrity and character.

Attribute #2: Personal Accountability

Personal accountability means to be responsible and answerable for the choices you make. The choices that you make reflect bits and pieces of your character. Your character has been cultivated for years as a result of your official and unofficial mentors, which are in your environment, family, peers and many other factors that now define who you are.

When you take this package called "You" into the marketplace, your employer expects you to produce. They have invested time, money and training in you. They are paying for your services during an eight-hour period. Your skills and abilities happen to fit into the objectives of the corporation. The corporation hired you based on your ability to perform, not on your good looks, or skills as a do-nothing conversationalist. Your ability to perform is measured by a performance review instrument. Your supervisor uses this instrument to assess the quality of your work based on specific indicators such as excellent, good, fair, and poor. These quality indicators assess your production and ability to meet or exceed the underlining standards for which the company hired you.

Attribute #3: Self-improvement

A company brings you in as a skilled or unskilled raw recruit to join its work force. You are there solely to increase the profit potential of the company. If managers felt by hiring you the company would not be profitable, then they would not have hired you. To hedge their confidence in you, they expect you to improve in your duties as you make improvements in your life.

While you are employed, your employer wants you to take advantage of in-house training and educational opportunities. Getting additional education and training increases your value in the eyes of your employer.

Attribute #4: Productive Attitude

Your attitude at work is your most important accessory. Being positive about your work shows up in your work, demeanor, and communications with other employees and clients. If you are self employed, your attitude is as important as food and water are to living. If you conduct yourself with a productive attitude and with a purpose to serve in your business dealings, your fortunes will increase. The company will reward you by giving you steady performance bonus increases. As a business person, your clients will reward your productive attitude by giving you repeat business.

Attribute #5: Work Quality

Nothing is more satisfying to your employer than for a job to be done right the first time. The one thing that is consistent that I have noticed in a job well done is quality. Invariably, work quality is identified as an attribute of something which is a masterpiece or good workmanship. When a job is done right the first time, the client is happy and the employer makes a profit. When the work is done poorly, the client is not satisfied and it costs the employer to redo the job. Poor craftsmanship may cost you your job; therefore, do it right the first time!

Attribute #6: Job knowledge

After a reasonable time, your employer expects you to master your job, being able to do it accurately and efficiently. Therefore, it is imperative for you to take the initiative to know the job inside-out. Often, your work is required to mesh with other mechanical components or business ventures which, when completed and combined, ends up being a total unit. If you are an entrepreneur, your clients expect you to be an authority on the subject. The client is relying on your job knowledge when you are contracted to design his or her project. With your knowledge, you must be willing to go beyond what is expected to get current data which will be of use in your design.

Attribute #7:
Conduct

All employees are expected to conduct themselves in a professional manner. Respect for others is the medium of exchange among professionals. No one has the right to impose his or her selfish will on another person. That is why proper conduct is important in the workplace. The work environment must be free from sexual harassment, bigotry, etc. If you don't know the code of conduct at your office or business, go over to your human resource center for that information.

Attribute #8:
Safety

You are hired as a primary worker for a task, and the company needs you to think about safety first. I was employed at a company that prided itself in the number of accident free days the work force had amassed. Every employee saw the updated accident free tallies as they entered the facility. As employees, we were aware of safety because the administration felt that it was important. I can not attest to the company's motives for emphasizing safety other than its desire for safety. The company wants its employees to be well and fit to carry out their duties on the job. Safety is a big concern in practically all business dealings.

Attribute #9:
Cooperative

Are you cooperative? That question can be best answered by your co-workers. Co-workers know whether you have built a relationship which makes them willing to work with you. Cooperation will come as a part of team work. A team will work together to achieve production goals. The individuals on the work team are motivated by pride in the quality of their work and the money they receive is recognition for their efforts. Good communication and respect breed a cooperative work environment. When people respect you, and you respect them, you will get cooperation.

Attribute #10:
Initiative

Initiative is the ability to act on your tasks, dreams or goals without someone having to tell you to do so. An individual must be willing to become proactive in life by taking the initiative to make his or her dreams a reality. If individuals are not willing to act, they must give assistance. When working with these individuals, you must be willing to trust them until they trust themselves.

Often, a job may require creativity. However, it's difficult to assign a creative job to someone who does not have self-confidence. Self-confidence is the key for taking initiative.

I have worked with people who were trained to do a job but needed prompting on every turn. These people were lacking initiative because of low self-esteem. Low self-esteem causes a person to do unwarranted reverification or second guessing of their decisions.

Attribute #11:
Attendance

You can't earn money for the employer or yourself if you don't showup. When your job attitude is good, your attendance is good. Your attendance really shows your attitude about your job. When the job becomes important enough, you will be present and on time. Not being motivated to come to work or arrive on time can be a sign of complacency or a need for a career change.

Attribute #12:
Honesty

In business dealings, before there is a contract to carry out a project, your financial backer will only do business with you because you are a person of character. As an entrepreneur or an employee, you are being rewarded because you are a trustworthy in your dealings. You are rewarded for your efforts in the form of a paycheck. Therefore, it is imperative that you work diligently and put great effort into your duties to help make the employer profitable. The employer had faith and trust in you enough to allow you to use the company's facilities, resources and instruments of the trade.

Attribute #13:
Reliable

If you say that you are going to do something or be somewhere, can you be counted on to do so? People who are reliable are consistent in their words and deeds. Business owners and customers are looking for reliable people. You are an important linkage in your employer's business enterprise. The employer is looking for consistent work-related behavior which makes a person reliable. When the employer finds qualities such as reliability and consistency concerning your work assignments, you will be rewarded for it.

CHAPTER 12

Being Tenacious in all Pursuits

Being Tenacious

When life gives you a lemon, make lemonade," is an old concept that I applied to my "Texas Nightmare." The ultimate reality of this concept helped me to overcome this painful adversity.

"When you want success as much as you want to breathe, you will have it" is a paraphrase from a story I read. I've learned that when you don't give much life to the words "can't" or "quit," you become tuned in to your dreams. Like the hound dog on the chase for the rabbit, the briars the trees, or the rivers do not matter to the dog. On the other hand, to a person pursuing a dream the problems, challenges or the adversities should not matter.

The purpose of my work today is to inform individuals that even though adversities or barriers will be their companion on their journey to their dreams, the manner in which they respond to adversities or barriers will ultimately determine their destinies. I believe if people can understand that success lies just beyond the problems, they might continue until they have succeeded. And if our young people can be exposed to the attitude of successful people, they will assimilate their attitude, virtues and live life successfully.

Life is always waiting to see how we respond to the struggles that are presented to us. When you are presented with a difficulty in life, tackle it with unparalleled determination to succeed.

Someone said, "Action is evidence of your faith." Every time you make a decision to move forward in the face of adversity, you are moving up your mountain. Everybody has his or her own mountain to climb. Yours will not be an actual mountain; instead, it will be a problem or an adversity that you are struggling to overcome.

When you succeed in climbing a mountain to your current dream, you must be prepared to start the journey over again. Because of obstacles, your dream will seem like it is on top of a mountain, but be not deceived. Challenges will test your worthiness to acquire your dream. You should continue climbing until you reach the summit of your mountain. At the summit, the only thing left to possess is your dream and plant your flag of conquest.

Just Believing

It takes faith to pursue your goal. When you have succeeded in accomplishing the goal, it no longer takes faith because you are in possession of the goal. The push that gets faith going is belief. Belief must be present at the onset of your faith journey. Belief gets the whole process going.

Parents rely on home training to protect their children when they go out into the world. What they are most concerned about is the protection of their children from hurt, from the influence of crime and from other negativisms of society. During these times, young people are looking for excitement or meaning in their lives. Therefore, they are vulnerable to exploitation of every kind. The void in their lives can be filled by simply trusting in God and oneself, doing the right thing, establishing close family ties and creating lasting friendships.

If you want to own a nice car, create a vision of the car, set goals and go out and work for it. On the other hand, those youth who have not learned to do this will see the car and go out and take it from someone. The magic is belief, a belief that you can make it happen —legally.

Before you can believe that the dream can occur, you must have the proper self-image to buttress your belief. A healthy level of confidence and self-esteem are two main ingredients that must dominate your self-image.

Your self-esteem dictates how much confidence you will have.

Your self-esteem evaluates your current level of self-worth to see whether you believe you are worthy enough to have the object of your belief. If a negative self-esteem deems you are not worthy of the object of your dreams, it will sabotage your efforts and success. There is conflict within. At the conscious level, you want the dream, but at the subconscious level, you don't believe that you deserve it.

Transformation occurs when you believe that you can achieve the object of your dream. You must change the way you imagine yourself to be from the inside out. You have got to believe that you are worthy. Your attitude regarding your self-worth has to change. The way I changed my attitude, which changed my poor self-esteem, is by realizing that God made me in his spiritual image. I believed that we are spirits, spiritual beings housed in physical bodies. I understood that the Spiritual Intelligence, God, is a spirit. This Spiritual Intelligence created everything that is physical or everything we can perceive with our five senses. Because of this attitude, you should not feel inferior to the skin pigmentation of another person.

God wants His word to influence the spirit of people for benevolent purposes. The free will of people drives them to do good or evil to produce or act according to their choices. In most religious books, the word of God is written to shepherd people in a path leading to doing His will—the will of the universal spirit of good.

It takes working on your self-esteem to gain the confidence needed to believe. In the words of Billy Florence of Amway, "You have got to believe that the great thing can happen". Before the great thing, the dream, will happen.

Your strategies have to be bent on changing the self-image. When I was on my journey to change my self-image, I believed in God's love and in my inheritance from Him. We are made in His spiritual image and should not feel inferior to anything in creation. I learned to incorporate the five attitudes for success in conjunction with some well-targeted affirmations to strengthen me where I was weak. It is how you view yourself that prevents you from acquiring the object of your dreams. When you have worked to transform the mental view of yourself, then your faith will begin to work for your good.

Achieving Ignited by Faith

Faith causes you to set your sights on higher realities which are responsible for motivating you to achieve your dreams. Faith keeps you going when you can't seem to go any more. Faith is the spark of energy that is always in reserve when you call on it. Faith has encouraged some people to decide to live and to get up from their death beds.

If you want to become successful in any endeavor, your faith must be greater than the adversity at hand to succeed at overcoming problems. Once you have struggled and climbed the mountainous barrier in your life, there must be movement toward multiple dreams which will benefit you and others. The message to learn from life's difficulties is to move forward with a dream plan, overcome any adversity and fulfill your purpose to serve.

In a physical sense, the sun is the source of energy for every living thing on earth. Everything relies on the sun for its energy. Essentially, we are energy dependent animals—acquiring our energy from food sources.

If we are energy dependent beings, where does the sun gets its source of energy? There has to be or had to have been a source even for the sun. I realize that the type of energy that maintains the sun has a scientific explanation. Yet, if you have a fire, something has to start it. Who started the sun to shine? Better yet, who ignited the spark that caused the theoretical big bang which is credited for causing the birth of the universe? It was the "Spiritual Intelligence," God. God is that spark of energy on which our faith is based!

God, as the basis of our faith, inspires us to be tenacious and hopeful when we are encountering difficult problems. I heard a minister say this concerning how the secular man views faith, "The secular man calls faith taking a risk. But, we as Christians call it faith." It's hard being tenacious when there is a zero percent chance of acquiring the object of our hope. So an informed person will have faith within the realm of things that God will act on. God will not be a coconspirator in anything that is evil which is outside of the realm of His blessings. If it is God's will, anything can be asked for in prayer and achieving it is possible.

This is why people have faith. It is because of who is the "solid rock" of their faith—the Author and Finisher—Almighty God!

Extending Success Into the Twenty-first Century

When I wrote this book, my goals were to explain how I was able to break through my greatest barrier—the "Texas Nightmare"—and to educate others. And I wanted to educate people about my system and the spiritual foundation that shaped my attitude toward the circumstances. My intent was not to bring an indictment against anyone or any system, but rather to reveal my story in an uplifting and inspiring manner, using the five attitudes for success that enabled me to remain strong.

I have always been an inquiring person. My love for science led me to study Engineering Technology in college. In my spare time, I enjoy reading scientific magazines. I love scientific information which attempts to explain the origin of the universe. I am also interested in learning about the multitude of physical phenomena which exist in the universe. My purpose in studying the universe is to understand the origin and nature of humans, and other organisms and objects within our environment. Scientists use a similar line of thinking. It is thought that by getting to know nature, we can better understand human beings.

I have come to believe that you have got to first understand the inner person before you can understand the universe. It is well known that the earth and the other planets orbit around the sun. The gravitational pull of the sun holds the planets captive. The planets are subjected to the influence of the sun. If the sun allows the earth to stray off its normal orbit, slightly, disasters will occur. Therefore, the earth operates best by staying in its orbit. The planets are under a strictly ordered orbital path around the sun. People are under the influence of natural laws. People who are sane and moral are capable of choosing to do the right thing. They orbit, consistently around their habits, and are eventually controlled by their habits. These habits cause them to become habit dependent—the saving grace is that these habit-dependent people can break their addiction; it starts with having a desire to do so. When you are in control of the habits for which you orbit, you can control, to a degree, your time, events, feelings, beliefs, actions, attitude and destiny. You use self-discipline to control your actions and events according to your dream plan. This is why one of the important things for a person to have is a dream of a future accomplishment.

When you envision yourself five years from now, how bright do you picture your future? If you see yourself successful and prosperous, you probably have a vision. A vision shows you the state of being that you want to exist in. Your vision includes your individual little dreams as well as the large ones.

I had a dream to earn a college education, but my thinking caused fear and negative thought pictures to be formed in my mind. A friend gave me the inspiration to eliminate those fears by simply encouraging me to take a step. He used my position of strength which is my ability to draw as motivation to get me to enroll at Denmark Technical College. This positive person was able to get me moving along my educational quest. My desire for this dream attracted me and caused me to focus my time and efforts toward its fulfillment. Therefore, in regards to achieving current and future dreams, I still have work to do.

In order for people to increase and improve their lives, they must be willing to invest in their personal growth. Every movement forward requires change. You must change to take advantage of the new opportunity. This is why you hear these words when you apply for a job, "I'm sorry you're not qualified or you don't have enough experience." To remedy the situation, you have to go out and become qualified and get some experience—this is change!

I have said before that adversities will be your companion along the road to achieving your dreams. If you realize that there will be adversities along the path to your dream, it would make sense to work on your attitude. Your attitude helps to keep adversities in their proper perspective and this is a stepping stone to success. Learn to take adversities under your control and not allow them to control you. When you are faced with problems, look at all angles to figure out how this experience can benefit you.

Fulfilling your purpose to serve others requires being productive. You have to be productive to obtain your financial goals and other aspirations. When you help other people, you should be experiencing a sense of fulfillment. Despite adversity, a sense of fulfillment is experienced because you have a purpose to serve others; you have a vision; you are committed to self-improvement; you overcome adversity and you are productive in your life. Look to the twenty-first century and employ the five attitudes for success and the character benchmark lessons to develop character and to negotiate adversity!

Appendix A

CHARACTER BENCHMARK: LESSON #14

List Dreams to Acquire

Write a minimum of 37 to 40 dreams on the list below that you want to acquire. They should be dreams that you want to accomplish during your life time. Below, the areas of one's life have been divided into six headings. List the appropriate dreams under the proper heading.

Don't be concerned about how large or small the dream is, how much it costs, or whether or not you can afford it. If it appears on this list, you may not currently have the money to acquire it. Once you have accomplished a particular goal, strike it off the list. If at any time you discover that there are others dreams you want to add to your list, do so at any time.

Dream List

Educational Dream List

1. ______________________________
2. ______________________________
3. ______________________________
4. ______________________________
5. ______________________________

Spiritual Dream List

1. ______________________________
2. ______________________________
3. ______________________________
4. ______________________________
5. ______________________________

Family Dream List

1. ______________________________
2. ______________________________
3. ______________________________
4. ______________________________
5. ______________________________

Income and Work Dream List

1. ______________________________
2. ______________________________
3. ______________________________
4. ______________________________
5. ______________________________

Career and Business Dream List

1. ______________________________
2. ______________________________
3. ______________________________
4. ______________________________
5. ______________________________

Health Dream List

1. ______________________________
2. ______________________________
3. ______________________________
4. ______________________________
5. ______________________________

Recreational Dream List

1. ______________________________
2. ______________________________
3. ______________________________
4. ______________________________
5. ______________________________

Volunteer Dream List

1. ______________________________
2. ______________________________
3. ______________________________
4. ______________________________
5. ______________________________

Appendix B

Parents, legal guardians, mentors and others may reinforce and assist youths in accomplishing a select number of the following enrichment and exposure activities by utilizing playacting or field trips, watching videos, listening to speakers, reading books, having discussions, reciting affirmations or listening to tapes.

100 Activities for Youth Success and Character Development

1. Make a list of 20 goals desired.
2. Distinguish the differences between goals and dreams.
3. Visit a successful sales organization.
4. Set 5 goals and accomplish them.
5. Study successful activities produced in great businesses.
6. Learn to utilize affirmations.
7. Develop a plan of action for every goal.
8. Write every goal down on paper.
9. Take action immediately on a desired goal.
10. Learn what moral price is necessary to accomplish your goals.
11. Read books or listen to tapes on the principles of goal setting.
12. Set goals to improve your spiritual activities.
13. Read from a book daily.
14. Execute the activities needed to fulfill your dreams on a 30 day cycle.
15. Examine the habits of successful people.
16. Visit city hall or the zoo.
17. Visit a junior college, technical school, college or university.
18. Visit local, state and national museums and libraries.
19. Visit the Grand Canyon or the Red Wood Forest.
20. Visit the Statue of Liberty.
21. Visit the Nile River in Africa.
22. Visit the National Aeronautics and Space Administration (NASA).
23. Visit Disney World, Six Flags and etc.
24. Visit a homeless shelter or a Salvation Army facility.
25. Visit your state capitol and the nation's capitol.
26. Visit tourist attractions in your state.

27. Visit a prison.
28. Visit a fire department.
29. Visit a police department or sheriff department.
30. Visit a military training facility.
31. Visit the Mayor's office.
32. Visit a county jail.
33. Visit a legislator or congressperson from your district.
34. Visit the spiritual house of your choice.
35. Visit a nursing home.
36. Volunteer to help out at a homeless shelter.
37. Volunteer to sing songs at a nursing home.
38. Volunteer to pickup trash in your community.
39. Volunteer to register people to vote.
40. Volunteer to repair the home of less fortunate persons.
41. Study United States history and world history.
42. Study anger negotiation skills.
43. Study conflict resolution skills.
44. Study different cultures.
45. Study the self-image profile of successful people in your nation.
46. Determine key weaknesses of racism and hate.
47. Determine the strengths that it takes to respect other people.
48. Determine the motivations of people who are "givers."
49. Determine the motivations of people who are "takers."
50. Determine ten effects of crime and violence in the community.
51. Read Martin L. King's story.
52. Read Abraham Lincoln's story.
53. Read Colonel Sander's story.
54. Read Les Brown's story.
55. Read Dexter Yeager's story.
56. Read Napoleon Hill's story.
57. Read Rosa Park's story.
58. Read Andrew Carnegie's story.
59. Read Alex Haley's story.
60. Read Harriet Tubman's story.
61. Reflect on positive resolutions to conflicts.
62. Reflect on positive thoughts.
63. Associate with law abiding peers.
64. Associate with people who respect authority.
65. Associate with people who avoid illegal drugs, gangs and crime.
66. Associate with people pursuing dreams and goals you desire.
67. Discover reasons to become more patriotic toward your country.
68. Invite a holocaust victim or historian for discussion.
69. Invite a slave historian for discussion.

70. Invite a victim of crime to discuss the effects of his or her ordeal.
71. Don't drag your feet when you walk.
72. Say thank-you when someone does something kind.
73. Give eye contact when talking to another person.
74. Live by family values based on virtues.
75. Register to vote.
76. Believe in yourself.
76. Believe in other people's security, respect and honor.
78. Treat people as if they are important.
79. View yourself as being unique.
80. Think on things which are good, great and loving.
81. Pay the price for success.
82. Become gainfully employed.
83. Study money markets, mutual funds, stocks and bonds.
84. Use computers to explore the internet for research, news and data.
85. Ride a train or fly in an airplane.
86. Adopt the concept of self-sufficiency.
87. Learn how to forecast problems before they arrive.
88. Become a student of your history and culture.
89. Learn to play golf.
90. Learn to play tennis.
91. Go to basketball or football events
92. Go on a camping trip to the mountains or forest.
93. Join a track and field team or basketball or football team.
94. Avoid violent television programs
95. Produce a system to improve your behavior and grades
96. Wear your clothes neatly.
97. Practice speaking standard English.
98. Graduate from every educational opportunity you pursue.
99. Go fishing.
100. Take a long walk on the beach.

Appendix C

Youth Character and Educational Pledge for Personal Change

I will be known as a person who is: kind, cooperative, studious, friendly, a team player, a hard worker, a constructive thinker, goal orientated, polite, honest, and dependable. If I am found violating this pledge, I will abide by the corrective actions that my caretaker, parent(s), mentor administers.

I am willing to change; therefore, I:
am non-confrontational;
express appropriate behavior;
am willing to apologize;
am prepared for class or meetings at all times;
talk only when it is appropriate;
do not offend others;
follow the instructions of my parents or teachers;
am concerned with earning good grades;
am only influenced by my positive dreams and aspirations;
abide by the rules of the school, home and etc.;
must earn an education before I achieve most of my goals;
am peaceful and I have a genuine concern for friends and family;
respect persons of the opposite gender;
have many dreams and goals to pursue;
encourage my peers;
have a drug-free attitude;
have a cooperating and compromising spirit;
respect myself and the rights of others;
am aware of my culture, current events, and identity; and I
expect to receive no negative referrals for the current school year.

I will write my signature as proof that I am willing to change.

____
Student or youth

I will support his/her effort for change and self-improvement.

____
Parent(s), mentor or legal guardian

Glossary

AFFIRMATIONS - Positive statements that are verbalized, and visualized (involving all five senses in the visualization process, if possible) for the purpose of influencing the mind to change or conform to suggestions.

ATTITUDE OF POVERTY - Those who have conditioned their minds for scarcity-dominated thoughts.

ATTITUDE OF PROSPERITY - People whose thoughts are conditioned to thinking in terms of abundance.

BARRIER - An unwanted hindering obstacle occurring in life.

BLOWING OUT THE FIRES OF CONFLICT - Getting disputants to avoid fighting, to calm down, to think clearly and to talk in order to resolve their differences.

CLAIMING - Spiritually taking ownership through faith of something desired or not currently in existence in life.

CAREER GOAL - An employment objective to pursue in a person's professional, governmental or business life.

CONFLICT RESOLUTION - An attempt to solve a disagreement between people with opposing viewpoints in a mutually beneficial manner.

CONSEQUENCES - The effect (what happens) of a decision already made.

CULTURAL AND IDENTITY AWARENESS - Deal with discovering and learning cultural pride, cultivating, and teaching the heritage of one's culture.

DREAMS - Desires that individuals are seeking to fulfill.

DREAMS DESIRED - Goals that inspire people to have something, to be more, and to do more to become their best.

DELAYED GRATIFICATION - Being disciplined to put off for later something that delights or gives pleasure.

ENVIRONMENTAL ATTITUDE - The opinions of people in the home, community and country regarding other people, things, places and events.

ENVIRONMENTS OF SUCCESS - Conditions which are highly conducive for achievement.

ENVIRONMENTAL THOUGHT PICTURES - The prevailing thinking in the community where an individual resides.

FAMILY VALUE CLARIFICATIONS - The principles in which parents or legal guardians believe are to be clarified and to be explained to family members.

FAMILY VALUE STRUCTURE - A belief and moral framework strong enough to support family members during problems, as well as encouraging competency to handle worst-case life scenarios.

FORECAST THINKING - Having the ability to anticipate the actions of people with positive or negative character.

GOAL - An specific objective which is meaningful, definite and measurable that people desire as part of their lives.

LAW OF REPETITION - Recurring thinking patterns, either positive or negative, that shape beliefs and habits.

LIVING BY EXAMPLE - People from the community or nation whose lives are exemplary and a prototype of virtue.

MAKING A DIFFERENCE - Volunteering to provide a benefit for someone without selfish motives.

MENTOR - A person of trust who acts as a guide to lead someone to the right path.

NEGATIVE INPUT - Unfavorable information from any source which is received and internalized. The information suggests bad, ugly, unqualified and unflattering attributes about a person or people.

NETWORKING - A cooperative venture between people for the sole purpose of income diversification or information exchange.

OUTPUT BEHAVIOR - The acts of individuals stemming from all sources of input, which forms their thinking, beliefs, attitude, feelings and actions.

PATRIOTISM - Deep-seated pride, love and support for one's own country.

PHYSICAL CONFLICT AVOIDANCE - An attitude of not wanting to be engaged in a physical altercation with another person—by skipping the fight and starting the communication process.

POSITIVE ATTITUDE - An attitude of hopeful thinking in which a person believes that what he or she wants in life will occur.

POSITIVE IDENTITY - Having a healthy identification and opinion of oneself or what one is capable of achieving.

PSYCHO-CULTIVATION - Principle used to acquire a serving and productive state of mind. It is becoming your best through the process of uprooting, changing and replacing of negative thought pictures by psychologically nurturing and acting on the following attitudes: to have a purpose to serve others and to provide skills and talents, to act on a vision, to improve oneself through personal growth, to overcome adversity and to become productive in life.

PSYCHOSOCIAL MODELING - A useful strategy in countering undesired behavior by responding properly to social dramas through playacting or role-playing.

PRODUCER - A person who provides a benevolent and beneficial service or product.

PRODUCTIVE STATE OF MIND - A useful frame of mind which benefits the person and others.

SELF-ESTEEM - Confidence and belief in one's abilities are determined by one's level of self-worth and efficacy.

SELF-INPUT - Information internalized and believed about one's self.

SELF-LEADERSHIP - Taking control of the personal leadership of one's life and the direction or path one has chosen.

SERVING - The act of sharing and providing skills, talents and knowledge for the good of humanity.

SERVING THE RELATIONSHIP - When two or more people are gathered together for mutual benefit, in peace or conflict.

SPIRITUAL INTELLIGENCE - A name or term for God.

SUCCESS - Having desired outcomes in an organization, business or one's life.

THE POWER TO REBUKE - Expelling undesirables with the belief and authority of God.

THOUGHT PICTURES - Mental images that are visualized in your imagination.

TAKERS - Those whose sole purpose is to serve themselves by stealing what others have produced.

VALUE FENCE - A value fence helps to cultivate moral boundaries in life. The positive core beliefs, virtues, attitudes and the direction a family believes constitutes an individual's boundaries.

VISION - Goals and dreams are two key components which makeup the multitude of pieces use to form the total picture of the things desired.

WORD OF GOD - One's religious scriptures (i.e., the Bible is called the Word of God).

YOUTH SUPPORTER - A person who gives assistance to teens or young adults.

YOUTH STRUCTURE - Virtues or values which are the framework of a youth's moral belief system.

Index

Symbols

A

B

C

D

E

W

Y

Bibliography

Greene, Cathy. Poem. Nothing Too Difficult. South Carolina: The Marzinza Publishing Group., 1995.

McCartney, Scott. "Former Co-Workers rally to jailed man's defense." Associated Press, 4 Dec. 1983.

Martine, Debra. "Wade reconsiders Geter case." The Dallas Morning News, 13 Dec. 1983.

Martine, Debra. "Geter freed after court OKs new trial." The Dallas Morning News, 15 Dec. 1983.

Babington, Charles., Jeff Brown., Bill Turque and Richard S. Dunham. "District attorney to seek Geter's release." Dallas Times Herald, 28 Dec. 1983.

The Open Bible Expanded Edition. Nashville, Camden & New York: Thomas Nelson Publishers, 1983.

United States. Dept. of Justice. Civil Rights Division. Reports under the Freedom of Information Act. Washington: GPO, October 1988.

Thomas, Paul G. Advanced Psycho-Cybernetics. New York: The Putnam Publishing Group, 1992.

Boy Scouts of America. Handbook for boys. Texas: Boys Scouts of America, 1976.

Carothers, Merlin R. Prison to Praise. California: Merlin R. Carothers, 1970.

About Lenell Geter

Lenell Geter—author, motivational speaker, consultant—has traveled from coast to coast to share his methods for developing a winner's attitude and, most importantly, freedom from Self-limiting confinement which leads to doubt, poor self-image, and low goals. Using methods, which are directly transferable to one's life, Lenell's "Five Attitudes for Success" enable families and individuals to overcome adversity and to lead successful lives. But why should you listen to Lenell Geter?

In 1982, Lenell faced what every person fears: he lost his freedom when he was arrested, convicted, and sentenced to life in prison for a crime he did not commit...even though professional colleagues corroborated his whereabouts when the crime occurred. He credits, "faith in God" as aiding in his withstanding the cold, cruel, and dangerous life in the Texas Department of Correction.

In pursuit of justice, family members and coworkers held fund-raisers, met with attorneys, and persuaded the media to pay attention to his plight. During Lenell's 16 months of incarceration in a maximum-security facility, the NAACP, local media and CBS'S *60 Minutes*—among others—investigated and uncovered evidence leading to Lenell's release and vindication by the state of Texas. On February 3, 1987, CBS aired *"Guilty of Innocence: The Lenell Geter Story,"* a major motion picture for television depicting the circumstances that led to his wrongful incarceration and his personal victory...a victory won out of faith, determination and the strength of his principles of life.

As the author of *Overcome, Succeed and Prosper*, Lenell has shared his "Five Attitudes for Success" across the country and has risen to become a motivational speaker of national acclaim. He is a member and professional speaker with the National Speakers Association. He is frequently honored for his talents and abilities and has received the Key To The City from several areas where he has worked.

Lenell has appeared as a guest on CBS, NBC and ABC television networks; he has been written about in People Magazine, Lawyer Magazine, Texas Monthly, Jet Magazine and scores of newspapers. He has also appeared on ABC's *Nightline* with Ted Koppel and the NBC *Today Show*.

Lenell Geter has earned a degree in Mechanical Engineering Technology; however, he is now positively engineering people to have faith and to believe that they can overcome self-limiting confinement. He is ready today to share his insights...at colleges and universities; he tells students that "obstacles will be their companion on the road to achieving their goals and dreams; however, the manner in which they respond to those challenges will ultimately determine their destinies." Lenell and his wife, Marcia Geter, reside in South Carolina with their three daughters: Marquita, Nzinga and Zakiya Geter.

To Book Lenell Geter As Your Next
Inspirational Speaker,
Call 800-232-3504 or 803-699-0327.

Website: www.lenellgeter.com
Email: info@lenellgeter.com

Order Form

Phone Orders: 1-800-232-3504 **Fax Orders:** 1-803-699-1497
Email: info@lenellgeter.com **Website:** www.lenellgeter.com

Mail Orders: The Marzinza Publishing Group
P.O. Box 24194
Columbia, SC 29224

Payable in U.S funds. No Cash orders accepted.
Please allow five working days for delivery.

Please send me ______ copies of **Overcome, Succeed and Prosper** at a price of $15.95 per book plus shipping and handling to the address below.

Payment by check:
___ Enclosed is my check

Mail product to: (Company or Individual)
Name: ____
Address: ______________________________________
City: __________________ State: __________________
Zip: ___________ Telephone ( ) __________________

Sales Tax:
Add 5.0% to total(South Carolina orders): $ _________
Shipping & handling:
Add $4.95 for the first book and $1.50 for each additional book:
$ __________

Grand Total: $ __________

Sales Tax:
Add 5.0% to total(S.C. orders): $ _________
Shipping & handling:
Add $4.95 for the first book and $1.50 for each additional book:
$ __________

Grand Total: $ __________